GW00385544

The Birth of British Rail

'Steam Past' Books from Allen & Unwin

THE LIMITED by O. S. Nock
THE BIRTH OF BRITISH RAIL by Michael R. Bonavia
STEAM'S INDIAN SUMMER by George Heiron & Eric Treacy
GRAVEYARD OF STEAM by Brian Handley
PRESERVED STEAM IN BRITAIN by Patrick B. Whitehouse
TRAVELLING BY TRAIN IN THE EDWARDIAN AGE by Philip Unwin
MEN OF THE GREAT WESTERN by Peter Grafton

By the same author:

The Economics of Transport
The Organisation of British Railways

The Birth of British Rail

Michael R. Bonavia, MA, PhD, FCIT

London
GEORGE ALLEN & UNWIN
Boston Sydney

Northamptonshire
Libraries

385

First published in 1979

This book is copyright under the Berne Convention. All rights are reserved. Apart from any fair dealing for the purpose of private study, research, criticism or review, as permitted under the Copyright Act 1956, no part of this publication may be reproduced, stored in a retrieval system, or transmitted, in any form or by any means, electronic, electrical, chemical, mechanical, optical, photocopying, recording or otherwise, without the prior permission of the copyright owner. Enquiries should be sent to the publishers at the undermentioned address:

GEORGE ALLEN & UNWIN LTD
40 Museum Street, London WC1A 1LU

© Michael R. Bonavia, 1979

British Library Cataloguing in Publication Data

Bonavia, Michael Robert
The birth of British Rail.
1. British Railways – History
I. Title
385'.0941 HE3020.B 78-40560

ISBN 0-04-385071-5

Picture research by Mike Esau
Book designed by Design Matters

Typeset in 11 on 12 point Imprint by Bedford Typesetters Ltd
and printed in Great Britain
by W & J Mackay Limited, Chatham

Contents

List of Illustrations — *page* 9
Author's Preface and Acknowledgments — 11
1. Transformation Scene — 13
2. The Tasks and the Men of the Hour — 23
3. Companies into Regions — 32
4. Liveries and Train Services — 42
5. Traction Policy — 52
6. The Carrying Stock — 70
7. Accidents and Incidents — 78
8. The Rank and File — 86
9. Ships and Sealing Wax — 91
10. The End of the Beginning — 97
A Note on Sources — 105
Index — 106

Illustrations

1	Four months after nationalisation	*page* 14
2	The death notice of the Companies	16
3	Sir Cyril Hurcomb	19
4	The new green livery	20
5	How 'Fougasse' viewed the new organisation	22
6	The Rt Hon. Alfred Barnes and Sir Eustace Missenden	24
7	No. 222 Marylebone Road	27
8	Advertisement for the Hotel Great Central	29
9	Still essentially 'Southern' in character	33
10	Cheshire Lines Committee rolling stock at Watford	34
11	Devons Road shed, 1949	35
12	Still very 'LMS' in 1948	36
13	Unrepaired war damage at Eastbourne station	38
14	The new liveries on the Great Central line	40
15	The lion and wheel totem	43
16	Eastleigh shed, 1951	44
17	'The Elizabethan' passing Peterborough	45
18	'The Cornishman' traversing Lansdowne Junction	46
19	The up 'Granite City' express leaving Aberdeen	47
20	The non-stop 'Devon Belle' changing engines	48
21	'The Royal Wessex' passing Clapham Junction	49
22	No. 70023, 'Venus', hauling the 'Capitals United Express'	50
23	Former station nameplates awaiting replacement	51
24	The locomotive exchanges of 1948	53
25	The final Castle class to be built	54
26	Prototype main-line diesel-electric locomotive no. 10000	56
27	The opening of the Rugby Locomotive Testing Station	56

28 The last LNER express passenger locomotive design 58
29 Ivatt D3 4–4–0 no. 2000 59
30 Gas turbine locomotive no. 18000 60
31 Fell main line diesel-mechanical locomotive no. 10100 61
32 Southern orthodox electric traction 62
33 Diesel main-line traction on the Southern 62
34 Southern unorthodoxy 64
35 Leader class no. 36001 65
36 First BR Standard steam locomotive 66
37 BR Standard light-weight 4–6–0 mixed-traffic locomotive no. 75006 67
38 BR Standard class 4MT 2–6–4T no. 80013 67
39 Before the wires reached Southend 68
40 The experimental electrification of the Lancaster–Morecambe–Heysham section 69
41 Exterior of 'At the Sign of the Three Plovers' 71
42 Pullman luxury 71
43 Interior of 'The Jolly Tar' 72
44 Prototype BR standard Mark I coach 73
45 Experimental double-decker coach 74
46 A motley collection of elderly freight wagons 75
47 The BR standard 24½-ton mineral wagon 76
48 The East Coast floods of 1948 79
49 The Harrow accident of 1952 80
50 King George VI's funeral train 82
51 British Railways Automatic Warning System 84
52 ss *Princess Victoria* 85
53 The School of Transport 88
54 ss *Brighton* 92
55 ss *Amsterdam* 95
56 A new era for British Railways 98
57 The Kelvedon–Tollesbury branch 99
58 Coaches no. 60462 and no. E62261 100
59 Star no. 4036 101
60 A Pullman special on 30 May 1953 102
61 A Midland Compound arriving at Chester 103
62 A4 Pacific 60007, 'Sir Nigel Gresley' 104

Author's Preface and Acknowledgments

British Railways or British Rail? Neither is in fact a statutory or legal title. 'British Railways', as a trading name for business purposes, was adopted by the Railway Executive of the British Transport Commission which took over the four main-line railways (and fifty-four smaller 'railway undertakings') on 1 January 1948; whilst 'British Rail', strictly speaking, was born only when the British Railways Board, then in control of the business, changed to the shorter form under the new 'corporate identity' programme adopted in stages during the later 1960s.

But I hope no one will accuse me of being anachronistic if I deal, under 'The Birth of British Rail', with the early years of the nationalised railways but use the name in force at the dates of which I am writing. Had my title been 'The Birth of British Railways' there would have been a risk that readers might have expected yet another account of George Stephenson and the historic performances of the 'Rocket'.

It seemed appropriate to carry the story of the 'birth' as far as the year 1953. Those six years following the passage of the Transport Act, 1947 – the nationalisation Act – cover the whole life-span of the Railway Executive, the body originally set up to manage the nationalised railways, until it was displaced by the British Transport Commission in October 1953 – the Commission itself being replaced by the British Railways Board on 1 January 1963.

So this book deals with the stewardship of the Railway Executive and what happened on the railways during those six years. Some people, possibly including former colleagues who were active in the Executive, may feel that I have been rather severe in commenting upon that body and its record. Admittedly, wisdom after the event is fairly cheap. But even at the time many of the younger men, like myself, were unhappy at the way things were being handled. The Executive seemed to assume that railways were going to remain – as they certainly had been during the war and still were in 1948 – the backbone transport system of the country. The policies of those early years might have been appropriate in the 1920s; they did not constitute a good preparation for the sharp scaling-down in the railways' share of the nation's transport that started in the mid-1950s.

Had the Executive worked energetically towards a modern traction policy; had it developed the Freightliner concept; had it addressed itself seriously to staff productivity; had it designed better coaching stock and more modern types of freight wagon had all these developments been at any rate well under way after five years, things might have been much better in the 1960s. The Beeching exercise need not have been so precipitate; the organisation need not have been turned up side down; the slide into deficit need not have coincided so disastrously with the demand for more public money to modernise the system.

Nationalisation of transport in 1948 was in no sense a necessity, except as the redemption of a party election pledge. However, once it had taken place it offered the opportunity of constructing an integrated road–rail transport service, an opportunity which unfortunately was not seized. Instead, in the early years there was a concentration upon irrelevancies and a failure to re-calculate the proper objectives of the railways.

I do not suggest that all major decisions since 1953 have been perfect, but great efforts have been made, by and large in the right direction. They need not have been so long delayed, nor have been made difficult, had matters been better managed in the first six years.

Some people may nevertheless look back with pleasure to those early years on BR, when the railways were still paying their way (more or less) and steam dominated the picture almost as completely as it had done in the 1930s. Nostalgia is just a matter of which side of the coin one is looking at.

I am very grateful to Mr Geoffrey Freeman Allen for his permission to incorporate in this book some passages I have written under the Ian Allan imprint in my book *The Organisation of British Railways* and in articles in *Modern Railways* and *Railway World*.

I

Transformation Scene

At midnight on 31 December 1947, all over Britain the drivers of night trains sounded their whistles. People hearing the whistling might have assumed that this was merely the customary railway salute to the New Year; in fact, it was also signalling the death of the private Railway Companies and the birth of British Railways.

Ten days later, in what was then the BBC's Home Service, I gave a talk entitled 'On Company's Service' in which I tried to say an appropriate farewell to the Big Four – the Great Western, the London Midland & Scottish, the London & North Eastern (my own Company) and the Southern. Their individual characters and achievements were, almost overnight, becoming a matter of history; they were now merged in an entirely new body, known to the lawyers as 'The Railway Executive' but to the public simply as 'British Railways' – not yet shortened to 'British Rail'.

Since then, a whole generation has grown up to whom the Railway Companies are merely names in the history books, and to whom British Rail is part of the Establishment like the Post Office, sometimes praised, often criticised, but accepted as an element of the State-controlled apparatus. It is easy to forget that the last generation knew that railways could be independent and diverse in many ways – not just in Company names and the liveries of engines and rolling stock, but in their managerial, engineering and operating practices.

This was reflected in the attitudes of most railwaymen to Companies other than their own. Although competition had been almost eliminated before the war so far as passenger fare cutting and freight rate cutting were concerned, there was still keen competition to attract business by quality of service.

'On Company's service' – 'OCS' for short – had for a century been a talismanic phrase, enabling a railwayman to identify himself when challenged for walking on railway property, to send a parcel on railway business free of charge, and to obtain a cup of tea in a station refreshment room at a staff discount. Now it had become meaningless overnight.

One can easily exaggerate the claim that *esprit de corps* was better before nationalisation; but it is certainly true that most railwaymen believed their own Company's practices and standards were better than those of any other.

The engine whistles that blew that midnight marked an end to the political battle that had raged for some eighteen months over the railway nationalisation provisions in the Trans-

1. Four months after nationalisation. The 'Flying Scotsman' stands in chequered sunshine at Edinburgh (Waverley), headed by a Gresley A4, with a wagon of materials for the Chief Mechanical Engineer in the background.

H. C. Casserley

port Bill, 1946, which became the Transport Act, 1947. The thing had actually happened and it had to be accepted as a fact of life. But did the public who used the railways, as opposed to the politicians and civil servants who had drafted the Transport Bill, have any clear expectation of the results of nationalisation? Equally, what did the railwaymen – rank and file members of their trade unions – expect?

For a while there was not much visible evidence of the changeover that had been so bitterly contested. The first thing that passengers noticed was the legend 'British Railways' painted on the tenders of locomotives, and the appearance of notices at stations headed 'The Railway Executive' or, more puzzlingly, 'British Transport Commission'. Otherwise the railways seemed for a time to change very little. A few humorists refused to pay their fares, claiming to be now part-owners of the system; others suggested that the railways should be renamed 'Royal Railways' and have their locomotives painted in Post Office red.

The Companies had died overnight, but their replacement, the Executive, was still, even to most railwaymen, a shadowy organisation. Some began to wonder why exactly the railways had been nationalised.

It seems rather an academic question today;

it happened so long ago, and in any case railways are State-owned in practically every major country in the world apart from the USA. The anomaly in fact may have been the survival of our private Company-owned systems as late as 1947. But anomalies need to be explained, and until the Second World War many people would have argued that the British railway Companies were on the whole more efficient than State railways anywhere else. The French nationalised their main-line railways completely only in 1938; and in the USA nationalisation has remained a dirty word even though the Federal Government has been forced into some drastic steps to assist the run-down railways of the Eastern States.

The argument about nationalisation of the railways had had a long history. Gladstone provided for the State to purchase all subsequently built railways in his famous 1844 Act, usually called the Cheap Trains Act because it was the first charter for the third-class passenger. But it remained a theoretical proposal (the nationalisation provisions of the 1844 Act were never implemented), putting its head up at intervals during the next hundred years. It eventually became a component of Labour Party official policy in which public ownership of 'the means of production, distribution and exchange' was to be spearheaded by nationalisation of fuel, power and transport as basic public utilities.

Neither of the two Labour governments before 1945 had had an overall majority enabling them to force through legislation of such a controversial kind. But the July 1945 general election, giving the Attlee Government a majority of 146 in the House of Commons, ushered in the series of nationalisation Acts that effectively turned Britain from a basically private enterprise economy into a mixed economy. Railways were swept into the bag of the 'public sector' along with coal, electricity, gas and the Bank of England. They were not even treated as a separate industry but were lumped together with London Transport, canals and road haulage as part of a future 'integrated' system of public inland transport.

The unions had for a long time supported railway nationalisation. The Trades Union Congress published in 1945 a report on *The Public Operation of Transport* which was widely accepted within the Labour Party as following and developing Socialist thinking on transport which had first been defined by Herbert Morrison (later Lord Morrison) in his pre-war pamphlet of 1938 entitled *British Transport at Britain's Service.*

The Morrison theme, based largely upon the author's experience as Minister of Transport in drafting the 1933 Act which created the London Passenger Transport Board, was that competition between different forms of transport was wasteful and did not lead to overall efficiency. Monopoly, provided it was publicly owned, could be more economical and serve the nation better. So there should be some kind of National Transport Board controlling the railways, long-distance road transport and certain other forms of transport.

The TUC pamphlet proposed a form of organisation – a central National Transport Authority with seven operating boards covering not merely railways, road transport, canals and ports, but also coastal shipping and internal air services – which was even more comprehensive than that which was eventually provided in the Transport Bill, 1946.

The argument underlying the political proposals was derived partly from the 'road–rail problem' that emerged during the inter-war years. Road competition had eroded the financial position of the railway companies,

SR
TRANSPORT
ACT 1947
GREAT WESTERN RAILWAY COMPANY
LONDON MIDLAND & SCOTTISH
RAILWAY COMPANY
LONDON & NORTH EASTERN RAILWAY COMPA
SOUTHERN RAILWAY COMPANY
LONDON PASSENGER TRANSPORT BOAR
Notice is hereby given that in pursuance of the abov
Act the Undertakings of the above named bodies vest
the British Transport Commission on 1st January, 194
and that on and after the said date all Byelaws, Regulatio
and Notices published by any of the said bodies and
operation immediately before the said date and all ticket
consignment notes and other documents issued or used o
and after the said date and which bear the name of an
of the said bodies shall be deemed to be published an
issued by and in the name of the Railway Executive
the London Transport Executive (as the case may b
constituted under the said Act.
BY ORDE
31st December, 1947

2. The axe has fallen: a railwayman at Charing Cross station reads the death notice of the Companies.
Keystone

who complained that they were unfairly restricted by statutory restrictions on their charges which did not apply to their competitors. In 1938 they had launched a so-called 'Square Deal' campaign, seeking legislation to relieve them of statutory controls originally imposed during their days of transport monopoly; and in 1939 the Government announced that the railways would obtain the relief they asked for, subject to certain safeguards. The Ministry of Transport began to draft the necessary Parliamentary Bill but the war intervened and the whole proposal went into cold storage.

By 1942, however, attention began to be paid to post-war planning in almost every major government department. In December 1942 Sir Cyril Hurcomb, Permanent Secretary of the Ministry of War Transport, wrote a long paper on the co-ordination of inland transport, which did not come down firmly in favour of any particular solution, but suggested that some form of Public Control Board as a co-ordinating agency might have advantages. By August 1943 Sir Cyril had developed his ideas and in a further paper he envisaged a 'co-ordinated scheme (whether it be based on unification or ownership or some pooling of receipts or some other means of exercising central control) for . . . the main line railways . . .'.

On 8 October 1945, barely three months after the Attlee government had taken office, a meeting on transport policy was held at 11 Downing Street under the chairmanship of Herbert Morrison, Lord President of the Council. The Minister of War Transport, Alfred Barnes, said he favoured separate boards for each form of transport that might be nationalised, rather than a National Transport Commission as had been suggested, because 'this would involve the building up of a machine that would be more powerful than the Ministry itself'. However, Morrison emphasised that Labour Party policy favoured the NTC concept.

Soon afterwards, on 22 October, a senior civil servant in the Ministry minuted that 'Railways, because of their relative and individual size and their present organisation and control, are obviously ripe for nationalisation'.

One may ask, why 'obviously'?

For a Commons debate on a censure motion on 5 December 1945, the Minister was briefed to say that 'there was no evidence that road and rail would produce any solution by voluntary co-operation' and that wartime experience had shown the need for 'effective central control and direction of our available transport facilities'.

An important paper drafted in the Ministry, also dated 5 December 1945, considered possible alternative types of organisation for nationalised transport: (1) regional (all forms of transport in a region to be under one authority); (2) territorial (based on the four main-line railways and using the railway organisations as the four branches on to which would be grafted the canals, docks and road transport); (3) functional (separate authorities for each form of transport). By 21 December opinion inside the Ministry had crystallised in favour of the functional system, apparently because it was felt that, as the paper argued, the territorial solution 'would tend to perpetuate the railway domination of road transport . . . it would arouse the road interests . . . to even greater fury'.

Meanwhile, on 19 November the Lord President had already announced publicly that 'powers will be taken to bring under national ownership the railways, canals and long-distance road haulage'.

The next twelve months were occupied in drafting the Transport Bill, which was first discussed in the House of Commons on Second Reading on 16 December 1946 and received the Royal Assent on 6 August 1947, coming into full operation on 'vesting day', 1 January 1948. The time taken to pass the Bill may seem lengthy, but even so the Government had had to apply the guillotine to its consideration in Committee, so that many clauses were never fully discussed. It was a mammoth piece of legislation, containing in its final form 170 pages, with 128 Sections and 15 Schedules.

Its development was steered by a Cabinet Committee, the Socialisation of Industries (Ministerial) Committee, chaired by the Lord President, with periodical progress reports to the Cabinet. The Cabinet papers are now open for scrutiny, and one can see that little interest was taken in questions of transport economics. In February 1946 the Minister of War Transport (his title became Minister of Transport later in the year) put outline proposals to the Cabinet for setting up a National Transport Commission with subordinate Executives for each form of transport to be taken over. His memorandum included this short sentence: 'I have rejected as impracticable and inexpedient – though it has some attractions – the solution of attaching all road, dock and canal undertakings to the main-line railway organisations in whose territory they now operate.'

Subsequently the Minister submitted the draft Bill first to the Socialisation of Industries Committee and then to the full Cabinet. One looks in vain for any estimate of the exact economic benefits to be obtained from these huge nationalisation proposals, or for any warning of possible disbenefits. Equally, there is no indication – apart from the sentence quoted above – that there were alternative forms of organisation that needed to be carefully assessed and put for decision before the Cabinet.

In fact, the aspects to which the Socialisation of Industries Committee and the Cabinet gave attention tended to be merely those where political or procedural difficulties might arise. Much care was devoted to ensuring that the Bill would not be 'hybrid' – a mixture of a public and a private Bill – which would slow its passage owing to the need for petitions against it to be heard in Committee. Great anxiety was expressed about the possibility of the railway directors paying 'death-bed dividends' to the shareholders in a last fling before nationalisation; solemn warnings were drafted to explain that this would reduce compensation and might lay the directors open to penalties.

The draft Bill contained a provision that the new Transport Commission should control traders' 'own account' lorry transport, the 'C' licence vehicles, on journeys of over forty miles. The Prime Minister was worried about the strength of political opposition to this – the Co-Operative movement is reported to have been very hostile – and in fact it was dropped from the Bill. Otherwise the whole issue was treated as a closed one, and the only questions to be settled were those of timing and expediency.

After the Bill was introduced into the House of Commons, the Government spokesmen's speeches (to many of which I listened) were undistinguished. Party doctrine and dogma replaced factual analysis of the problems of the railway industry. Nor, it must be said, was the case for keeping the railways under private

3. The first day's work ahead; Sir Cyril Hurcomb, Chairman of the British Transport Commission, walks through St James's Park to his new office in 55 Broadway on the morning of 1 January 1948.

Keystone

4. In May 1948 Derby Locomotive Works is completing the painting of a locomotive in the new green livery, lined out in red, cream and grey, but with 'British Railways', and not yet the new totem, on the tender.

Keystone

enterprise put any better. Conservative speakers tended to concentrate on irrelevancies and showed no more grasp of transport economics than Ministers and Labour backbenchers.

In fact, the specific issue of railway nationalisation was submerged in the Labour Government's ambitious plan to set up a single huge corporation to control and manage all forms of public inland transport.

The Transport Bill provided that railway nationalisation was to be effected by the relatively simple process of 'vesting' in the British Transport Commission all fifty-nine railway undertakings listed in the Third Schedule to the Bill. (The number was so large because, in addition to the 'Big Four', practically all the minor railways and all the separately incorporated joint lines had to be listed.) The greater part of this huge Bill was concerned with the duties and powers of the British Transport Commission, the method of compulsorily acquiring road haulage businesses, the drawing up of charges schemes, the preparation of area schemes for road passenger transport and ports – intended to lead to an eventual complete State monopoly of these activities.

But nothing was said in the Bill, or in its later form as an Act, about just how the railways were to be organised under nationalisation, except that, whilst they would be owned by the Commission, that body would delegate the task of railway management to a subordinate body called 'The Railway Executive'. (The Executive always gave 'The' in its title an initial capital letter, but nobody else did!)

The relationship between the Commission and the Executive was peculiar. On the one hand, the Commission's activities were to constitute one business; on the other, the Railway Executive members were appointed directly by the Minister of Transport and *not* by the Commission, and it was laid down that the Executive was to be treated as the employer of the staff and, as a body corporate, to be entitled to sue and liable to be sued in law. A recipe for controversy as to who, in the end, was to be really in charge of the railways!

Obviously, one wonders why more practical experience was not drawn upon to devise an effective set-up for the nationalised British Railways. Early in 1946 the Minister met the Chairmen of the four main-line railway companies and invited their views on various matters including units of management, but the Chairmen shied away, preferring to wait until the Bill had been published. After the Bill had been published some contact took place on points of detail between officers of the Ministry and of the railways; but by then there was no possibility of co-operation over the basic form of organisation. This 'chicken and egg' situation was unfortunate.

Meanwhile the railway boards fought on against nationalisation. Before the war, a booklet entitled *Railway Nationalisation: an Impartial View* had been published reproducing a series of articles attacking nationalisation that had been sponsored by the LMS in *Modern Transport*. The arguments in this booklet were now refurbished and publicised in a stream of literature sponsored by the Railway Companies Association. The Association's role was important because it represented the boards of directors who were looking after the shareholders' interests, though the railway working was actually still, under the wartime Control Agreement, being run by the Railway Executive Committee of the Ministry of Transport. The money spent on propaganda against nationalisation had to be kept quite separate from the money passing through the Railway Control Account – the receipts and expenditure from the ordinary railway working.

5. How 'Fougasse' of *Punch* viewed the new organisation.

Punch

This did not deter the Companies. A Committee of General Managers' Assistants, of which I was one, was formed to direct the campaign. A costly public relations expert was brought in from outside as an adviser. Literature poured out, and a poster campaign was organised on the slogan 'Stop the Transport Bill'.

The LMS, who had spearheaded the pre-war 'Square Deal' campaign to free the railways from statutory restrictions upon charging, plunged happily into the controversy by drafting polemical pamphlets and challenging critics on the subject of the railways' record in peace and war. There was a certain irony in the fact that the LMS President, Sir William Wood, was soon to be designated as a Member of the future British Transport Commission!

Many of the younger officers felt that there was a certain unreality, an element of shadow-boxing about the campaign, having regard to the Government's huge majority and its election pledge to nationalise transport. It was, however, probably good tactics from the point of view of the shareholders' compensation. In the end, the shareholders were compensated on the basis of the current market value of their holdings, exchanged for British Transport stock, which on one line of reasoning was equitable and on another was unfair in that railway finances would have been far sounder had there been no Railway Control Agreement imposed by the Government during the war and had the Companies been allowed to retain their earnings from the swollen wartime traffic.

It was with very mixed feelings therefore that railway managers went to their desks on Thursday 1 January 1948. Some were hopeful; some sceptical; some cynical or depressed. None could have accurately foreseen what the future of the nationalised railways would be like.

2

The Tasks and the Men of the Hour

Like nations, industries pass through phases during which they throw up the natural leaders the situation requires, followed by other periods when no outstanding figures emerge and the second eleven seems to hold the field. In the early years of British Rail, the industry had lost the great railwaymen of the pre-war era, whilst the major public figures who took the stage later were still waiting in the wings. Distinguished General Managers such as Sir Herbert Walker, Sir Ralph Wedgwood and Sir James Milne had retired and Lord Stamp had been killed in an air raid. The emergence as national figures of Sir Brian (later Lord) Robertson and Dr (later Lord) Beeching lay in the future.

If there was a certain drabness about the years 1948–53, it started at the top. Alfred Barnes, the Minister of Transport who piloted the 1947 nationalisation Act through the Commons, was an uninspiring character. His promotion to Cabinet rank had been a reward for years of service in the Co-Operative movement. He had had no previous involvement in transport and merely stuck to the task laid down for him in the party manifesto and in the briefs written for him by his civil servants – treating the whole vast operation as a chore to be performed without complaint. Having said this, one must admit that Alfred Barnes was not easily shaken; he plodded steadily through the debates despite furious Conservative opposition and, in effect, did the job the Cabinet had told him to do. Small and undistinguished in appearance, he was nevertheless shrewd and could be quite tough. At a meeting with the trade unions he effectively deflated big Jim Figgins of the NUR who had been blustering and who clearly expected a Labour minister to give way when a major union thumped the table.

But it could not be said that Barnes – despite having no doubt consulted his Cabinet colleagues – was very clever in his appointment of the five 'wise men' who were to run the vast conglomerate of nationalised transport, unless age was to be the test of wisdom. Of the five full-time members, Sir Cyril Hurcomb (the Chairman) and Sir William Wood were both 64 and Lord Ashfield was 73. The only comparative 'youngsters' were Lord Rusholme, former General Secretary of the Co-Operative Union (57) and John Benstead, ex-General Secretary of the NUR (50).

6. At the controls. The Rt Hon. Alfred Barnes, Minister of Transport, and Sir Eustace Missenden, Chairman of the Railway Executive, in the cab with Driver E. F. Moore of King's Cross shed.

National Railway Museum

From the outset the Commission was far from being a happy band of brothers. It was very much a one-man band; at meetings the Chairman overshadowed the others, who normally only spoke if called upon. This was surprising because Hurcomb, who had been a brilliantly successful civil servant, and was regarded as a driver, impatient of delays, never gave the impression of enjoying the exercise of open authority or accepting public responsibility. He had for so long been accustomed, as a Permanent Secretary, to advise, inform and manipulate ministers from behind the scenes that he seemed uncomfortable at being in the limelight himself. He argued impatiently instead of directing; he had the Commission's minutes drafted so that instead of being simple records of decisions they contained homilies and self-justificatory explanations.

Former railway officers working for the Commission, accustomed to a clear-cut 'yes' or 'no' from a Board of Directors, read the Commission minutes with astonishment and inquired whom they were supposed to impress. The answer was of course that Hurcomb, from long training in the Civil Service, wanted the minutes to be on record if necessary in order to refute possible future criticism. He would frequently argue that a course of action was inadvisable because 'we shall be criticised if . . .'. To railwaymen accustomed to being criticised day in and day out, this seemed weak-kneed.

Hurcomb was a complex character. I wrote in *The Times* after his death that 'he was baffled by the obstinate independence shown by, at least, the Railway Executive. He shrank from issuing formal directives and instinctively felt that letters of reasoned argument, supported if necessary by harangues at meetings, must lead to co-operation and he was exasperated when this did not happen.'

If the Commission was virtually a one-man band, this may have been partly because the former race of railway tycoons was not effectively represented upon it. Sir William Wood, ex-President of the LMS, had been ill-advised to accept membership. He was quite unable to show any of his former effectiveness after losing the support of a large headquarters organisation. Lord Ashfield, who had dominated London Transport for forty years, was in his seventies and died only ten months after vesting day.

Lord Rusholme's very considerable administrative abilities – he disclaimed any special knowledge of transport – were not properly utilised by Hurcomb. The member whom the Chairman found most helpful in various ways, not merely for handling labour questions, was John Benstead, who not so long afterwards was promoted into the Deputy Chairmanship and a knighthood.

One ex-railway general manager, Miles Beevor, was not a member but served as Chief Secretary and Legal Adviser of the Commission. He had not had time to spread his wings before nationalisation, as he had only been Acting Chief General Manager of the London & North Eastern Railway. He soon became disillusioned with the Commission and after three and a half years resigned to take up a major position in private industry.

The Commission had a dynamic chief officer in R. H. (later Sir Reginald) Wilson, the Financial Comptroller. But he only emerged as a public figure later, after the abolition of the Railway Executive, when he became a BTC member, Chairman of first the Eastern and then the London Midland Area Board, and eventually Chairman of the Transport Holding Company and of the National Freight Corporation. In the early years following the birth of British Railways he was too heavily occupied with the mammoth task of sorting out the Commission's complicated finances to emerge as a public figure.

So there were no real giants in the period covered by this narrative. What a pity! If, for instance, the Chairman of the Transport Commission and the Chairman of The Railway Executive had been temperamentally fitted to work together as a team (of which there are good examples in railway and transport history, such as Sir Ralph Wedgwood and Robert Bell on the LNER, Lord Stamp and Sir William Wood on the LMS, Lord Ashfield and Frank Pick on London Transport), how much happier and more effective would have been these crucial early years after 1948. On the contrary, there was poor liaison from the outset between 55 Broadway (meaning the BTC's two upper floors in the London Transport building, which Hurcomb was persuaded by Lord Ashfield to accept as a suitable headquarters for the most comprehensive if not the largest transport undertaking in the world), and the former Great Central Hotel in which the Railway Executive had installed itself with some attempt at shabby dignity.

The contrasts were striking, in both accommodation and personalities. The Commission's status as a lodger in the less desirable portions of one of its own Executives' premises was anomalous. The main benefits were that Lord Ashfield need not vacate the sumptuous chairman's room that he had occupied for so many years, and Sir Cyril Hurcomb need not leave the purlieus of Whitehall in which his career had been chiefly made.

The Railway Executive had, even before vesting day, set itself up in 'shadow' form in the Great Central Hotel, now officially rechristened No. 222 Marylebone Road, and unofficially dubbed 'The Kremlin'. The hotel had originally been built for (but not by) the Great Central Railway, which was desperately short of money after its mammoth exertions in building a trunk line from Nottingham that would enable it to run into London. Every major terminus was considered to need an hotel, and the money for the Great Central had been put up in 1899 by a syndicate headed by Sir Blundell Maple, the financier and friend of Sir Sam Fay, General Manager of the GCR. The hotel was a good example of the style adopted for many large buildings in the *fin de siècle* period. The public rooms were huge; staircases were designed for giants; there were stained-glass windows and a winter garden where afternoon tea was served to the accompaniment of a string orchestra. But it had a reputation for solid comfort and good if unexciting meals; it was also very reasonably priced and was liked by Sheffield businessmen who used the Great Central route into Marylebone and by housewives from Amersham or Chorleywood who enjoyed a Winter Garden tea between shopping in the West End and catching the train to their Chiltern homes.

The hotel was not, however, a great financial success, partly because it fell between the standards of the true West End, where prestige could justify high prices, and the cheapness of the nearby Bloomsbury establishments. When war came it was closed to the public and requisitioned by the War Office; it served as a transit centre for troops – mainly from overseas – passing through London.

Although escaping major war damage, the building was very dilapidated by the end of the war. The London & North Eastern Railway purchased it for £500,000, intending to use it to replace offices which had suffered bomb damage, especially at King's Cross Station. Permission for office use was however refused by the Government and the hotel was temporarily occupied as a hostel for trainmen

7. No. 222 Marylebone Road in later days, but still very little changed in exterior appearance from its time as the Great Central Hotel.

British Rail

needing to stay overnight in London. The approach of nationalisation induced Whitehall to change its mind; permission was given to use the hotel as the headquarters of British Railways, none of the Company offices being available or suitable for that purpose. Work started on the building in the autumn of 1947 and continued intermittently for thirty years until the decision was finally taken that the whole building must be re-modelled. Its only real advantage for office use was that, being a former hotel, the provision of lavatory accommodation was more generous than is normal in offices!

In this edifice the Railway Executive's Chairman, Sir Eustace Missenden, presided over the members as *primus inter pares*, but not as chief executive. Each member went his own way, developing his own ideas – usually flavoured strongly by his former Company's practice.

Missenden gave many the impression of being cold, but he was intensely loyal to the Southern and he supported those who had been close to him and upon whom he could rely. He had been only the second choice for the post, after Sir James Milne of the GWR had declined it. And in the subsequent wheeling and dealing to fill the other positions it had been thought necessary to give each former main-line Company a fair crack of the whip; this did not necessarily mean that the best talent available could be drawn upon in every case. And a function applying to British Railways as a whole would naturally be coloured by the outlook of the member responsible, whilst the headquarters staffing would probably be mainly drawn from that member's former Company colleagues or subordinates.

Dealing with the functions in turn, commercial matters were placed under David Blee, formerly Chief Goods Manager of the Great Western Railway. These matters included continental traffic of which the GWR experience was the smallest of all among the Companies.

Railway operating, shipping and docks came under the taciturn, strong-willed 'B-W', otherwise V. M. (later Sir Michael) Barrington-Ward, formerly Divisional General Manager of the LNER. Mechanical engineering, electrical engineering, road motor engineering and scientific research were placed under R. A. Riddles, formerly a Vice-President of the LMS. Research was no doubt included in the Riddles portfolio because the LMS was the only company with a research establishment of any consequence.

Civil and dock engineering, signalling and telecommunications (and architecture!) were put under J. C. L. (later Sir Landale) Train, formerly Chief Engineer of the LNER.

Staff and establishment, welfare and medical services came under a member drawn from the unions – 'Bill' (W. P.) Allen, former General Secretary of ASLEF, the Associated Society of Locomotive Engineers and Firemen.

The 'odds and ends' – public relations and publicity, estate and rating, the railway police and stores departments – were put under a very distinguished appointee as Deputy Chairman, General Sir William Slim, later Field-Marshal Lord Slim. He quickly endeared himself to his colleagues on the Executive but after ten months resigned on his appointment as Chief of the Imperial General Staff, being succeeded on the Executive by General Sir Daril Watson.

The new Railway Executive had simultaneously to keep the railways running at a very difficult time and to remodel the organisation. The Government seemed to expect that nationalisation would automatically relieve the physical problems created by poor mechanical

LONDON

HOTEL GREAT CENTRAL

Favourite Rendezvous for Travellers from the North

Close to the Terminus of the Great Central Railway, enjoying all the delightfully fresh air of the Regent's Park and adjacent heights, yet within a few minutes of the Marble Arch, Hyde Park, and other fashionable centres of the West End as well as Club and Medico Land, the Art World, Lord's Cricket Ground, and Madame Tussaud's

LIGHT AIR HEALTH COMFORT

INCLUSIVE TERMS: from 15/- per Day

For a stay of not less than One Week

Designed to afford all the comfort and refinement of a well-ordered mansion without its attendant anxiety, and also without extravagant outlay. The spacious central courtyard secures grateful seclusion to arriving and departing guests, gives light and air to every room, while the terraced footway surrounding it provides a pleasant promenade

ORCHESTRA IN WINTER GARDEN
MAGNIFICENT PUBLIC-ROOMS ELEGANT PRIVATE SUITES
BEDROOMS WITH BATHS ATTACHED
RESTAURANT RENOWNED CUISINE

DECORATION AND FURNISHING BY MAPLE

BROCHURE ON APPLICATION TO MANAGER

Telegrams:—"Centellare, London" G. SCHMEIDER

'A TEMPLE OF LUXURY'

With Tariff more moderate than any other Hotel of the same class in London.

8. Bargain offers! An advertisement for the Hotel Great Central in the GCR timetable for 1903.

Author's collection

condition of engines, insufficient and poor quality coal supplies, wagons needing repair and structures deteriorating through wartime neglect. Rationing was still in force, not merely of food and clothing but of coal, steel, timber and other basic materials for industry. The railways came off badly in the allocations they were given; the Government view was that they could 'live off their fat' for a little longer. The fact that the fat had melted away in the war years never seemed to penetrate the official mind.

During the war the unified operation of the railways (while still Company-owned) under the Railway Executive Committee had certainly effected economies through common use of rolling stock and central control of operations. So nationalisation could not of itself immediately throw up very much more in the way of additional savings. The real need was to re-equip the railways, if they were to carry on effectively.

The early years of British Railways were bedevilled by uncertainty as to where the real centre of authority lay. At the top the British Transport Commission presided over the heap of transport businesses that had been 'vested' or 'acquired', trying to make sense out of the obligation to 'integrate' them; immediately below the Commission, the Railway Executive pursued its own policies for unifying the former Company systems and establishing a single national railway; lower still, in the Regions where many Company traditions were preserved, the Executive's attempts at standardisation were often resented and opposed.

To the Commission, the Executive appeared too inward-looking, bent on restoring the railways to something like their pre-war condition, rather than to enabling them to play a new role in an 'integrated' and up-to-date transport system. The Commission's pressure on the Executive to work towards road–rail integration was met by taking purely token steps such as the establishment of a joint conference with the sister Executive, the work of which proceeded at a snail's pace.

The Railway Executive's attitude was, not altogether unreasonably, that it had its hands full for the time being in coping with current traffic problems and reorganisation. In this it was tacitly supported by the Road Transport (later Road Haulage) Executive. Neither in fact wanted a shotgun wedding service, to be conducted by the Commission.

In the long run this was a disaster for the railways. Had there been a swift move towards Regional road–rail transport units under the Commission – a development at which Alfred Barnes had hinted to the Cabinet as being a likely form for a future organisation – railway finances might have been better and the public might have had better service.

But functional Executives there were and they closed the ranks against interference. Missenden was the last chief executive of the railways who was able to adopt the railwayman's traditional attitude to politicians and civil servants – that of the expert telling the amateur, more or less politely, not to meddle with matters he does not understand. He was a highly professional and competent if unimaginative traffic officer whose transition from the acting to the substantive post of General Manager of the Southern Railway, while his predecessor was temporarily on Government wartime service but still below retiring age, had caused some raised eyebrows. Although he had accepted the chairmanship of the Executive he gave the impression that he disliked both the principle of nationalisation and the organisation of a functional Railway Executive acting as the agent of the British Transport Commission. Brought up in the managerial tradition of Sir Herbert Walker, but now bereft of the controlling role of a General Manager, Missenden cannot have relished the spectacle of his functional Executive members going their own way (or forming temporary cabals among themselves to get it). Equally, he undoubtedly resented the presence of the British Transport Commission as intermediary between the railways and the Ministry. Temperamentally, he and Hurcomb were poles apart. His irritation flared up once on receipt of a BTC letter signed by Hurcomb about shipping services, when he added a handwritten line at the bottom of the Executive's formal reply: 'P.S. We do *not* call our cross-Channel steamers "boats".'

The members of the Executive were given direct authority over the departmental officers in the six Regions which had been carved out of the Railway Companies. The following sentence in RE Instruction No. 2 to the London Midland Region clearly sets out the position. 'Instructions as detailed later will be given direct to the regional departmental Officers by the Member of The Railway Executive concerned, just as reports will be made direct by the regional departmental officers to the appropriate Member of The Railway Executive.'

The new generation of leaders in the six railway Regions were thus told plainly that they were *not* to be General Managers but only local representatives of the Executive, co-ordinating the work of the departments and settling purely local issues. So from the start there was some tension not only between the BTC and the Railway Executive but also between the Executive and the Regions.

3 Companies into Regions

Whilst controversy and policy arguments were rife at the top of the organisation, the problems being faced and the decisions being taken by the Railway Executive and the Commission were very remote from the men who manned the trains and stations or maintained the track. They were remote, too, from anything that passengers or traders using the railway noticed for quite a long time.

It was after all in the Regions that the railways existed in any real sense. The Regions had overnight replaced the Companies but for some considerable time continued to perpetuate Company practices. At the outset each Chief Regional Officer (there were no General Managers) came from the predecessor Company, and the team of officers who worked in the old Company offices usually shared the same origin and traditions.

The Executive decided to attack excessive 'Regionalism' by moving senior officers from one Region to another. 'Divide and rule' seemed a good way to enhance Executive authority by weakening Company traditions. In this it was only partly successful; many of the 'foreigners' adopted the practices of their new Region with enthusiasm, and advocated them as strongly, if not more strongly, as those who had grown up with them. Nowhere was this more the case than on the Southern, where the unseen influence of Sir Herbert Walker seemed to linger indefinitely at Waterloo.

To paint a word-picture of each of the Regions a very large canvas would be needed. But a quick tour may give some impression of how British Railways carried on at working level after nationalisation. The Executive in its circular instructions addressed the Regions alphabetically, and it is appropriate to begin with the Eastern. However, as the Eastern and North Eastern Regions shared, for a number of years, joint departments and were so intimately associated in the East Coast Main Line train service, it is convenient to discuss them together.

The North Eastern existed only by virtue of a last-minute decision to give it Regional status. Originally it had been intended that the whole of the LNER apart from Scotland should (as in the case of the LMS) form one Region – a position to which a return was made much later when the two Regions were amalgamated in 1967, under the British Railways Board. On nationalisation there was some rejoicing amongst the railwaymen at York at achieving Regional status, reflecting the past glories of the North Eastern Railway before it became merely an Area of the LNER. The ghost of George Hudson might have been heard repeating his slogan 'Mak' all t'railways cum t'York'.

However, as the LNER in its area organisation (under which a Divisional General Manager at York had enjoyed great authority) had excluded various 'all-line' departments, including those of the Chief Engineer, the Chief Mechanical Engineer, and the Chief Accountant, these departments continued to serve the two Regions jointly for some years.

The Eastern Region headquarters was in the ex-LNER Southern Area offices at Liverpool Street, where the Chief Regional Officer sat in the oak-panelled General Manager's office of the former Great Eastern Railway. The CRO was C. K. Bird, a brilliant intellect and a very capable railwayman unfortunately dogged by ill-health in the years before his death in 1958. This forced him to delegate very extensively. But the loyalty of the Eastern Region Officers to 'C.K.B.' was unquestionable and the traditions of the LNER were fiercely maintained at Liverpool Street.

The Southern Area of the LNER had

9. Still essentially 'Southern' in character in 1950: a Margate–Ashford–London train at Wye, headed by a Wainwright 4–4–0, retaining all its classical lines.

Derek Cross

10. An early result of nationalisation; Cheshire Lines Committee rolling stock in temporary use on services at Watford Junction.

W. Philip Conolly

comprised the 'Three Greats' – Great Northern, Great Eastern and Great Central Railways. There were three termini, each with former headquarters offices adjoining. So the Eastern Region departments were dispersed between Liverpool Street, King's Cross and Marylebone, at least until the Regional boundaries began to be re-drawn. One major boundary change took place early with the transfer of the former London Tilbury and Southern section of the LMS to the Eastern Region. There was perhaps some poetic justice in this. The former Midland Railway had snapped up this small but useful railway under the nose of the Great Eastern in 1912, which cost that railway's General Manager, Walter Hyde, who had not acted quickly enough, an enforced retirement at the age of 50.

At York the close-knit team who had served under C. M. Jenkin Jones, the brilliant but sometimes prickly Divisional General Manager of LNER days, welcomed another LNER man, C. P. Hopkins, himself born and bred in York, as Chief Regional Officer, even if some considered him a trifle young for such high office.

by bad luck. A disproportionate number of accidents seemed to take place on its system, and the tightly centralised control that had been exercised from Euston in LMS days was now transferred to the more remote Executive at 222 Marylebone Road. In fact, the London Midland Region was barely manageable in the way that smaller Regions were. Consideration was given to creating a separate North Western Region based on Manchester, but the proposal was dropped. Curiously, no real study seems to have been made of the advantages of splitting the Region into North Western and Midland components – as the operating and motive power functions had long been divided.

In contrast with the huge unwieldy London Midland Region, the Scottish Region emerged – surprisingly – during the period as entirely manageable despite the fact that it had been welded together from two former competitors, the Scottish portions of the LMS and the LNER. Under the lugubrious but very capable T. F. Cameron (former Divisional General Manager of the LNER at Edinburgh), now the Chief Regional Officer, the organisation took shape surprisingly quickly. The fine tradition of Scottish railwaymen no doubt helped and old rivalries seemed to disappear.

The Southern Region faced the post-war period with confidence. So much of its mileage was electrified that the problems of poor coal and inadequate steam locomotive maintenance were not so serious as elsewhere. The Southern Railway's close association with the Pullman Car Company had enabled it to restore some quasi-luxury services relatively quickly after the war. The process continued after nationalisation, with John Elliot's energetic personality as Chief Regional Officer ensuring that the Southern's brand of enterprise would not lose momentum.

It cannot have been altogether easy for his successor, C. P. Hopkins, to come from the North Eastern Region into such a close-knit family, steeped in a tradition of meeting special problems in a special way. His arrival was a consequence of Elliot's move to Euston and he was replaced at York by H. A. Short, a thoroughgoing Southern man. Many people considered such an exchange rather pointless. However, there would have been several Southern candidates for the Waterloo position whose noses would have been put out of joint by Short's appointment, and bringing in an outsider might be considered an adroit move in the circumstances. In any case, Hopkins once again identified himself closely with the team he was to co-ordinate if not to lead, and after a time people forgot that he had ever been an outsider.

Last in alphabetical order, but not in any other way, comes the Western Region. When in 1923 four Companies emerged from a process of merging 120 railways, the Great Western was the only one that preserved its previous identity, merely swallowing up some smaller railways including the Cambrian and the South Wales coal lines. This time (despite a gallant attempt to keep the GWR in being as a legal entity even though the railway network might be nationalised), the heritage of Brunel and Gooch passed to the upstart body at 222 Marylebone Road. The Western Region however maintained a brave face; the Chief Regional Officer, the outspoken K. W. C. Grand, had been Assistant General Manager of the GWR and the senior departmental officers at Paddington, some of them formidable characters, were not disposed to accept meekly any directives from the Executive members other than from their own David Blee who had taken several GWR officers to form his team at Marylebone.

13. The Southern soon after nationalisation, showing the unrepaired war damage at Eastbourne station on 3 September 1949. No. 2350 stands ready to leave with the 9.42 am to Birmingham (Snow Hill).

S. C. Nash

For the time being, the Executive handled the Western with kid gloves. The GWR had had an enviable reputation for safety and staff courtesy; it was popular with the public and the Conservative Opposition MPs saw it as a symbol of private enterprise unnecessarily and irresponsibly nationalised. Contacts between Paddington and Westminster were not entirely absent; as soon as the general election of 1951 returned a Conservative majority the Region's position was greatly strengthened, morally if not officially.

How far did the Regions carry on the characteristics, the policies and the projects which the predecessor Companies had bequeathed to them? The Companies had certainly not been idle between the end of the war and the vesting day. The Railway Companies Association had, through its Commission on Post-War Planning, proposed that it should become a statutory body dealing with all major railway policy matters; that the whole of the railways in Scotland might be worked as a regional unit; that the 'joint lines' should be transferred to one or other of the parent Companies; and that lines of one Company which penetrated into territory mainly owned by another Company should be transferred to the latter.

Much of this was translated into action after nationalisation. However, a good deal of Company planning, particularly in the traction field, was scrapped by the Railway Executive. The Southern Railway was committed in principle to the electrification of its remaining main lines in the central and eastern sections. It had also ordered two experimental 1,750 hp diesel-electric locomotives for comparative testing of possibilities elsewhere. The Great Western, always combining great conservatism in some matters with extreme progressiveness in others, commissioned two gas-turbine units, which had a short and chequered career. The LMS had ordered two 1,600 hp main-line diesels.

The LNER had even bolder plans. In 1945 the company had despatched H. W. H. Richards, its Chief Electrical Engineer, to the USA to study diesel-electric traction. His report, although cautious, suggested an extended trial in this country. In 1947 the Chief General Manager put forward a proposal, which the Board accepted, for replacing thirty-two Pacific steam locomotives on the East Coast services by twenty-five main-line diesel-electric locomotives. This project, unlike the part-completed Shenfield and Manchester–Sheffield/Wath electrifications, did not survive nationalisation. It was thus to be some twenty years before the Deltics could show how diesel traction could transform the East Coast Main Line services. No doubt the LNER scheme would have run into teething troubles, but a great opportunity to gain experience and accelerate the eventual changeover from steam was lost in the brushing aside of Company policy by the new Executive.

There was a great contrast in attitudes between those sections of the management remaining at Regional level, often using the former Company head offices, and inclined to uphold tradition and to value continuity, and those officers who had migrated to join the new Executive and in many cases were now issuing or drafting orders to their former colleagues. In extreme cases, those who had left to join the Railway Executive were called 'the traitors'. Those others – a very small band – who had left to join the British Transport Commission were regarded more with surprise and pity than resentment. The reason was simple: the Commission's officers were given little authority and were even (officially) supposed to have no contact with their 'railway'

14. The new liveries on the Great Central line; the 6.15 pm 'Master Cutler' leaves Marylebone on 21 July 1949 behind an A3 Pacific, now renumbered 60052 and bearing the new totem on the tender.

Ken Nunn Collection

colleagues except through official correspondence signed by the Chief Secretary and addressed to the Secretary of the Executive.

Occasionally, however, the organisation was by-passed and a Commission officer such as myself would be invited to lunch in a Chief Regional Officer's mess at Waterloo or Paddington. There the traditional trappings of a railway general manager's office survived. It has often been remarked that railway management retains a 'service' flavour – managers are classed as 'officers' and their luncheon room is a 'mess'. This may be a survival from the earliest days when railway Company Boards turned to the armed services to recruit their managers from the ranks of those accustomed to command and familiar with the problems of maintaining discipline.

On such occasions, after the mess waiter had served the after-lunch coffee, the conversation would often turn on the remoteness and arbitrariness of the Executive, its insensitivity to tradition and the local problems of the Region. Strongest in resisting encroachment was the Western Region under its uninhibited Chief Regional Officer, Keith Grand, who carried on the traditions of the old GWR. Its operating was old-fashioned and its utilisation of locomotives and stock poor by modern standards. Yet it had a splendid safety record; it had, alone among the Companies, installed a form of automatic train control on all its main lines; it had pioneered the widespread use of diesel railcars on routes of light traffic. Its locomotive fleet was its pride and joy, even though the design characteristics were basically half a century old; its passenger stock was a curious assortment of designs. Lastly, its staff morale and its public standing were probably the best of those in the Big Four.

The capacity of the Western Region to maintain under nationalisation the distinctive character of the GWR never ceased to surprise. A simple example is to be found in the design of semaphore signal. When, between the wars, the other three main-line Companies adopted the upper-quadrant design, which is lighter and simpler in construction than the former standard lower-quadrant, the Great Western adhered obstinately to the lower-quadrant. After nationalisation, when standards in all forms of equipment were being prescribed by the Executive, not one upper-quadrant signal appeared on the Western Region; indeed, when under the 'penetrating lines' elimination policy the Western acquired some sections of 'foreign' routes, any signals thereon needing renewal were – to the cynical amusement of detached observers – replaced by GWR lower-quadrant semaphores. Apparently an unlimited stock of lower-quadrant signal components had been built up before nationalisation!

So the 'virtues of variety' struggled against the forces seeking uniformity and centralised control and, British tolerance and love of individuality being what it is, were surprisingly successful for some time.

4

Liveries and Train Services

With what some people considered to be a concentration upon irrelevant details, the Railway Executive held, less than one month after vesting day, a 'beauty contest' at Kensington (Olympia) station to decide on the colours in which BR's locomotives were to be painted. Considering that no cleaning – or virtually no cleaning – of steam locomotives was then being undertaken, it may well have been thought that the colour of the paint underneath the grime would be rather an academic question.

At the 'beauty contest' four ex-LMS Class 5 4–6–0 locomotives were on show in three shades of green (GWR, LNER and SR) as well as one in the black livery lined out in red and white of the pre-grouping London & North Western Railway. In addition, an ex-Southern Railway electric locomotive was there in blue with silver lining. No prize was awarded at this parade, but just over two months later another parade was staged at Marylebone Station, across the road from the Executive's headquarters, to demonstrate the final selection of engine liveries – royal blue with black and white lining for what were termed 'heavy duty' express passenger engines; green for other passenger engines, with black and orange lining; and ex-LNWR black, lined, for other types. Handsome as some of these locomotives appeared when fresh from the paint shop, a few months in service reduced them to the grimy anonymity that had persisted during the war and post-war years.

Passenger rolling stock was less quickly dealt with. Great Western chocolate with cream upper panels was compared with experimental vehicles painted in what was reputed to be the former LNWR livery but which in fact failed to reproduce the true blackberry-black and off-white of that Company's rolling stock. Instead it well earned the designation 'plum and spilt milk' coined for it by a newspaper, and did not survive for long.

In early 1949 it was decided that main-line corridor coaches should be painted crimson lake, with cream upper panels. Vans and non-corridor coaches were to be crimson lake, unlined; multiple-unit electric stock was to sport the 'malachite green' of the Southern Railway, thus avoiding a massive change of liveries in the Southern Region. The official 'crimson lake' was far removed from the splendid deep colour of the former Midland Railway, and the popular name for the new BR livery, justifiably enough, became 'raspberry and cream' – a slight dietary improvement on plum and spilt milk.

15. The lion and wheel totem adopted for use on locomotives, showing the resemblance to the 'Wembley' lion of 1924.

British Rail

16. Officially BR but still very 'Southern' in character – the east end of Eastleigh shed in December 1951, with G6 class 0–6–0 30260, Merchant Navy class 35030, and King Arthur class 30803, all just out of the works.

Les Elsey

The effect of these livery experiments was strikingly illustrated when one day I saw the Newhaven boat train leaving Victoria headed by an electric locomotive in blue, followed by a bogie van in Southern green, several coaches in 'raspberry and cream', a Pullman car in umber and cream, ending with two bogie vans in crimson lake – five liveries in all.

While the Executive was looking at colour schemes for locomotives and rolling stock, the BTC was interesting itself in obtaining a 'totem' which could be applied not only on the railway but also on road vehicles and ships. Sir Cyril Hurcomb commissioned a design which was intended to be generally applicable, since it included the inevitable lion – to indicate national ownership – and a wheel which might have either a steel or a rubber tyre. On BR locomotives it appeared as a lion rather uncomfortably straddling a wheel through which ran a bar carrying the legend. The design had a vague affinity both with the famous London Transport 'bull's-eye' and with the stylised 'Wembley Lion' that had been the symbol of the British Empire Exhibition of 1924. I never heard anyone except Sir Cyril Hurcomb himself express any liking for this object, often rudely described by the staff as the 'bicycling lion' or the 'starving lion' in reference to its unfortunate attitude and its meagre physique. It was neither heraldically authentic nor artistically attractive.

Looking forward a few years, Hurcomb's successor, Sir Brian Robertson, soon applied to the College of Arms for a truly heraldic device which when it appeared repeated the lion-and-wheel formula but in a much happier juxtaposition; it survived until the late 1960s when it was replaced by the BR double-arrow logotype.

17. 'The Elizabethan' on the third day after its inaugural run, passing Peterborough on 1 July 1953 behind A4 Pacific no. 60009, 'Union of South Africa'.

Les Perrin

For its posters, station nameplates and staff cap-badges, the Executive designed its own 'totem' which was comprised of two elliptical shields, one superimposed on the other in a way that dimly echoed – once again – the London Transport bull's-eye. These twin sausages were quite innocuous if rather uninspired; they carried the words 'British Railways' against a different background colour for each Region. The Eastern was in deep blue, a colour that the LNER had favoured for its publicity. The London Midland, less happily, sported a muddy maroon shade that represented the ultimate downgrading from Midland red. The North Eastern was given a bright orange colour, the reason for which was never explained. The Scottish had a light, almost a Cambridge blue, which might have been based on the colour of the Caledonian Railway's engines. The Southern, inevitably was green, and the Western, equally inevitably, was chocolate.

The first improvements in passenger train services after vesting day had of course been planned as part of the companies' aim to restore railway services to the pre-war level but only came to fruition after the companies had been nationalised. The LNER was anxious to operate its famous streamlined train sets (officially known as the High Speed Trains,

18. Cross-country trains also bear names: 'The Cornishman' from Wolverhampton to Penzance on 25 May 1953 in charge of Hawksworth County class no. 1004, 'County of Somerset', traversing Lansdowne Junction, Cheltenham.

P. J. Lynch

19. The up 'Granite City' express leaving Aberdeen on 29 July 1953 behind BR Standard 5MT 4–6–0 no. 44980.

Brian Morrison

anticipating by forty years the use of this title by BR) but the vehicles had been dispersed and the track could not, owing to maintenance arrears, permit pre-war speeds being repeated. A start was made by reassembling the stock for the main East Coast services in the summer timetable of 1948, when the 'Flying Scotsman' resumed its non-stop running between London and Edinburgh, though at lower speeds than before the war. In the same year the 'South Yorkshireman' Marylebone–Sheffield–Bradford service on the Great Central Line was inaugurated, and a Pullman train to Newcastle ran as the 'Tees-Tyne Pullman'.

The 'Capitals Limited' – non-stop from London to Edinburgh – started to run in May 1949. On the Great Central the 'Master Cutler' – a name I had been responsible for originating in LNER days – continued to be popular with Sheffield businessmen.

In 1951 the Liverpool Street–Ipswich–Norwich service was reorganised to give London–Norwich journeys of 2 hours 10 minutes at standard departure times. This was possible through the allocation to these trains of Britannia type Pacific locomotives, the most successful of the BR standard designs.

Not until 1953 did any train run at speeds even approaching the best pre-war levels. But in the summer service of that year the non-stop 'Elizabethan' express performed the journey between London and Edinburgh in $6\frac{3}{4}$ hours – three-quarters of an hour slower than the pre-war 'Coronation', which moreover had two intermediate stops. It was however a heavier train. Also on the East Coast route the North Eastern Region in 1952 was operating the 'North Briton', from Glasgow to Leeds, at the fastest schedule then in force in Great Britain between Darlington and York, 44·1 miles in 42 minutes (63 mph – modest by today's standards).

On the West Coast route, the 'Royal Scot' began to run again between Euston and Glasgow in February 1948. In 1951 LMR cross-country services were improved, and named trains were increasing, including London–Liverpool and London–Manchester services, the 'Merseyside Express' and the 'Comet' respectively. However, problems of heavy train loading and difficulties with both track maintenance and mechanical maintenance in the Region exercised a damping effect on ambitions to speed up services.

Many of the Scottish Region's principal trains were Anglo-Scottish. The 'Queen of Scots' Pullman train from London via Leeds to Glasgow had restarted in 1948. But several expresses operated entirely within the Region acquired names in 1949. They were the 'Bon Accord', the 'St Mungo', and the 'Granite City' (Glasgow–Aberdeen); the 'Fife Coast Express' (Glasgow–St Andrews); and the 'Irishman' (Glasgow–Stranraer Harbour). Travel in Scotland during that period in fact could be very enjoyable if one took a splendid Scottish breakfast in the restaurant car and

20. The consequence of having no water troughs! The non-stop 'Devon Belle' has to change engines between Waterloo and Exeter, the selected location being Wilton, just west of Salisbury. Here the up Pullman train leaves in charge of Merchant Navy Pacific no. 35011, leaving the sister engine on the siding, on 26 July 1952.

Les Elsey

21. 'The Royal Wessex' passing Clapham Junction on 25 June 1951, hauled by West Country Pacific no. 34095, 'Brentnor', and ~~overtaking~~ passing 2-BIL electric unit no. 2142.

Brian Morrison

22. BR Standard designs arrive on the Western Region; an immaculate Britannia class 4–6–2 no. 70023, 'Venus', of Cardiff (Canton) Motive Power Depot, hauling the up 'Capitals United Express'.

W. Philip Conolly

noted the cleanliness of carriages and stations compared with those south of the border.

If progress towards extending the Southern's electrified mileage hung fire, there was plenty of enterprise where steam traction was concerned. The through Wagon-Lits sleeping-car service on the Dover–Dunkirk train ferry was restored between London and Paris just about the time of nationalisation, and in 1948 a new Pullman train, the 'Thanet Belle' came into service between Victoria and Ramsgate. The 'Atlantic Coast Express' to Devon and Cornwall ran in very much its pre-war order, with numerous portions for different destinations. The 'Devon Belle', a new Pullman train, ran to the same part of the country – it, together with the Bournemouth, Brighton and Thanet Pullmans, made up a quartet of 'Belle' trains on the Southern. In addition, there was of course the 'Golden Arrow' Pullman Continental service, revived after the war, but which gradually lost its prestige character as first-class travellers were progressively diverted to air.

In 1951 the Region experimented with a double-deck suburban train of ingenious design which was not perpetuated, mainly on account of the extra time required at stations for loading and unloading.

The Region in 1953 gave a name – the 'Man of Kent' – to a train from Charing Cross to Dover, Deal and Sandwich, an innovation for a non-Pullman train in the South Eastern Division. But in general, during the period the Region was too preoccupied with the problems of renewing the electricity distribution system and of lengthening suburban trains, with associated station platform lengthenings, to cope with increased traffic.

It had been a severe blow to the GWR when the fuel crisis of 1946–7 had forced the discontinuance for a time of the 'Cornish Riviera Express', the celebrated 10.30 am from Paddington. It returned however and was joined by the 'Torbay Express' soon after.

23. Redundant! Former station nameplates, in both Southern Railway and Railway Executive standard designs (the 'double sausage'), awaiting replacement.

Mike Esau

After nationalisation, the Western Region found that the condition of the track did not permit a restoration of the pre-war 'Cheltenham Flier' with its run from Swindon to London in 65 minutes for the 77·2 miles – a record in its day. However, in 1950 the Region introduced the 'Red Dragon', the first named train for South Wales, and in 1951 the 'Merchant Venturer' between Paddington and Bristol. Another South Wales named train was introduced under the title of 'Pembroke Coast Express' in 1953. But the list of individual named trains with a touch of glamour about them must not obscure the fact that progress towards a return to pre-war levels of speed was slow. The 1939 timetables had given Britain, it is arguable, the best passenger train service in the world for speed combined with frequency. The drastic slowings of the war period lingered on for years after peace had returned.

In 1951 some damaging comparisons were made between the current main-line services on fifty trunk routes, and those in force *not* in 1939 but in 1913, thirty-eight years earlier! If the comparison were made between 1939 and 1951, only two of the fifty routes had been restored to the pre-war level of speed – London–Brighton and London–Norwich. There were substantial improvements made in the summer timetable of 1954, just after the Executive had been abolished; but it was not until the 1960s, with electrification and diesel traction schemes coming to fruition, that the pattern changed dramatically for the better and the modern Inter-City type of service emerged on all principal routes.

5

Traction Policy

The Railway Executive's steam traction policy was a major factor in creating the unfavourable opinion of its management, which led to its abolition in 1953.

The Executive had inherited from its Company predecessors the following motive power units:

Steam locomotives (traffic)	20,023 (of 448 types)
Electric locomotives	16
Diesel-electric locomotives	53
Diesel railcars	40
Electric motor vehicles	2,006

The distribution of these resources over the Regions varied considerably; but for British Railways as a whole there was no doubt that, whilst steam was vastly the most important existing resource, it was precisely over the future of steam that the greatest doubts must exist. Abroad, in the USA there had been a massive changeover to main-line diesel traction; the European railways were rebuilding their war-shattered systems with heavy investment in electrification. In Britain the conditions in the coal industry and the labour market that had favoured steam traction had disappeared, probably for good.

It was therefore with some astonishment that, only four months after nationalisation, the BTC learnt of a Railway Executive decision to carry out large-scale inter-Regional locomotive exchanges, followed by the decision to build twelve standard new types of steam locomotives, of which six were to be inserted into the building programme for 1951.

This seemed to be a clear example of putting the cart before the horse. An overall motive power policy was surely needed before making a heavy investment in steam, especially since, allowing for the time required to design and build the new standard types, and for the normal life expectancy of steam locomotives, the Executive was assuming that steam would still be playing a major role on BR well into the 1980s.

With this in mind I drafted, the Chief Secretary of the Commission approved, and Sir Cyril Hurcomb signed, a letter to the Chairman of the Railway Executive asking that a committee should be appointed, upon which a representative of the Commission would sit, to report on the estimated future balance of advantages as between steam and the other forms of traction, primarily from the economic angle.

No action was taken by the Executive on this request for over eight months. Meanwhile, the steam locomotive exchanges continued and

24. The locomotive exchanges of 1948; on 20 May the 1.10 pm from King's Cross to Leeds, Eastern Region, leaves behind Western King class no. 6018. Note the dynamometer car behind the tender, and the spectators at the platform end.

Ken Nunn Collection

the plans were developed for designing new standard types. In December 1948 the committee was finally constituted – incidentally ignoring Hurcomb's request for BTC participation in its membership. The committee took nearly three years to report, by which time the programme for building standard steam locomotives had acquired considerable momentum.

The Commission chafed at all this but felt unable formally to direct the Executive to change technical decisions which seemed to lie within the scope of the scheme of delegation of powers to the Railway Executive.

It is certainly possible to argue that in 1948 a wholesale changeover from steam to electric and diesel traction would have been premature if not impossible. But it seems astonishing that, as E. S. Cox has narrated in *Locomotive Panorama*, on 1 January 1948 a team assembled in 222 Marylebone Road, committed to an extensive steam locomotive building policy before a full review of the alternatives had been carried out and certainly before the Commission's views on this major policy issue had been ascertained.

The Executive had of course inherited from the former major companies several locomotive building programmes that could not be halted immediately. Work was in progress, materials were on order. And in any case the state of the railways demanded immediate refreshment of the locomotive stock that had been overworked and undermaintained during the six years of war and the two and a half years since peace came.

1947 had been a year when post-war building by the Companies was beginning to get into its stride, even though – with the notable exception of the Southern – the locomotive types being built still reflected, despite modifications, the designs of the outstanding Chief Mechanical Engineers of the pre-war age. On the LMS Fairburn and Ivatt had followed Stanier, and Thompson and Peppercorn had followed Gresley on the LNER. Hawksworth had succeeded to the GWR tradition established by Churchward and Collett. On the Southern, exceptionally, there was a great innovator in the shape of that erratic genius, Oliver Bulleid. However, whilst Edward Thompson had changed many of Gresley's design characteristics, his stay had only lasted about five years; and Peppercorn had been much more of a Gresley man. So Stanier, Gresley, Collett and Maunsell (Bulleid's very able if less adventurous predecessor) were the great names attaching to most of the locomotive designs of the Big Four at vesting day.

There were problems for the Executive –

25. The last of a great line, in all her spotless glory; the final Castle class 4–6–0 to be built, no. 7037, appropriately named 'Swindon'.

British Rail

considering the individualism and entrenched authority of Chief Mechanical Engineers in Company days – in dealing with the present incumbents. They became Chief Mechanical and Electrical Engineers for the Regions that replaced their former Company systems. The loss of status must have been hard to bear. (Their successors did not include 'Chief' in their titles.)

Most of them did not stay long under the new regime. Peppercorn retired in 1950 and died in 1951; Hawksworth and Ivatt retired in 1949 and 1951 respectively; Bulleid left in 1949 and later joined Coras Iompair Eireann as Chief Mechanical Engineer where his fertile brain and the Irish climate combined to give birth to the concept of a peat-burning locomotive!

The successors of these men were J. F. Harrison, first on the Eastern and North Eastern Regions, and later on the London Midland Region; Kenneth Cook on the Western (and later the Eastern and North Eastern Regions); and S. B. Warder (an electrical engineer) on the Southern. Never having enjoyed the power of pre-nationalisation Chief Mechanical Engineers must have made it somewhat easier for the second generation to accept the downgrading of their posts.

How did the original ex-potentates react at the outset? E. S. Cox has written: 'It says much for human adaptability that they co-operated as well as they did, only shadowed by an often wooden demeanour when they faced us across the table at the monthly M and EE Committee meetings, and punctuated by occasional outbreaks of sheer naughtiness.'

There is of course something fundamentally wrong about any organisation in which headquarters complains about 'sheer naughtiness' in those who are supposed to execute its policies. There has been a failure to communicate and establish any sense of common purpose.

Riddles and his team were meanwhile proceeding with gusto to develop the new 'standard' designs for BR locomotives. I have put 'standard' in inverted commas, because so-called standardisation schemes often act in reverse – they merely add to the total number of types in service for which spares have to be kept and knowhow acquired – unless certain conditions are fulfilled. First, the inspirer of standardisation must be reasonably certain of a long period in office, and that his successor will not prematurely discard his policies. This, for instance, was not the case when Edward Thompson formulated his 'standardisation' plan for the LNER as he had only a short expectation of years in office. Next, a continuing demand for the type of motive power involved must be predictable for at least a quarter of a century, preferably longer. Lastly, there must be the financial resources clearly in sight for large-scale scrap-and-build, quickly replacing non-standard by standard products – as when Stanier took office on the LMS.

None of these prerequisites was present when the Riddles team plunged into their task. Of course, for some time the only locomotives that could emerge from the erecting shop would have to be existing Company types. It was in fact not until 1951 that the first BR 'standard' locomotives appeared – 89 compared with 208 of Company designs in that year, although in the following year the 'standard' types began to predominate.

The workshops at Crewe, Horwich and Derby on the London Midland Region were, on nationalisation, engaged in building the last two of the famous line of LMS Pacifics, Class 5 4–6–0s and Class 4 2–6–4T engines, as well as post-Stanier types designed by Ivatt for relatively light work. At Swindon, Castle Class

10000
L M S

SIR NIGEL GRESLEY
60007
46256

26. The LMS-English Electric prototype main-line diesel-electric locomotive no. 10000 on the 2.15 pm Manchester express at St Pancras on 17 July 1948.

W. Philip Conolly

27. The opening of the Rugby Locomotive Testing Station on 19 October 1948. The last of the great Chief Mechanical Engineers of pre-nationalisation days, with two distinguished visitors from France. Left to right, A. H. Peppercorn, O. V. S. Bulleid, Louis Armand, F. W. Hawksworth, Edward Thompson, M. Parmentier, Sir William Stanier, H. G. Ivatt.

National Railway Museum

4-6-0s, which had first appeared in 1922 but were still admirable workhorses, were being turned out, together with other orthodox GWR designs. Doncaster was building the first Peppercorn Pacifics; Darlington was building one of Edward Thompson's useful designs, the L1 2-6-4 tank, and private builders were producing more of Thompson's other successful design, the B1 4-6-0.

The Southern were building Bulleid's Pacifics, in Eastleigh works the larger Merchant Navy class and at Brighton the smaller Battle of Britain type. But the Executive had no hesitation in halting the programme for building the same designer's ill-starred Leader class tank locomotives for the Southern Region. The prototype had already demonstrated that the highly original thought embodied in the design of these unique machines had not taken into account a number of factors, including overheating of the cab to such an extent that drivers would be roasted. Considerable secrecy was maintained over this fascinating but foredoomed attempt to rethink the steam locomotive, and the units in course of erection were quietly scrapped.

There was certainly scope for studying in depth the strength and weakness of existing Company designs and discovering whether the 'horses for courses' principle really justified such wide variation as existed in design. This was a reason for the series of interchange tests from April to September 1948, which delighted railway enthusiasts. But basically (as E. S. Cox has remarked) they merely confirmed what most students had already suspected, 'that any locomotive designed on modern lines was as capable of running in Cornwall as it was in Scotland. Moreover, human differences in driving techniques could sometimes produce bigger variations on the same engine than those which lay between different engines driven in a like manner. There thus emerged no essential barrier in performance or efficiency to the introduction of standard locomotives for use throughout British Railways.'

The last sentence is perhaps debatable. Why, given what is said immediately before, were not the most effective Company designs selected and perpetuated until the emergence of a real traction policy, not necessarily bound to steam? This would have eliminated a vast amount of planning at BR headquarters and detailed design work in Regional workshops, as well as the retooling and building up of large stocks of spares.

The contrary argument could only be based on the assumption that the central design team could produce steam locomotives markedly better than the very best Company designs. Was this achieved? It seems doubtful. Some good principles were laid down, such as ease of maintenance and ability to steam freely

28. The last LNER express passenger locomotive design: Peppercorn 4–6–2 A2 Pacific no. 60528, 'Tudor Minstrel', of Dundee shed waiting to leave Aberdeen with the 9.55 am express to King's Cross on 24 July 1952. One of the last survivors of a class of fifteen, no. 60528 lasted until 1966.

P. J. Lynch

even with coal of indifferent quality. But, of the 12 BR standard types proposed in the middle of 1948 not all were built or even demanded by the Operating Departments; and the success of those types that were built varied considerably. The most appreciated were probably the Britannia 4–6–2 design – planned as a second string to a larger Pacific type of which only one was ever built – and the heavy freight 2–10–0 which proved to have an astonishing turn of speed despite its relatively small driving wheels and was successful in keeping time with express passenger trains.

Was there, in fact, a real Indian summer of steam traction? I fear not. If attention had been concentrated upon getting the best possible performance out of existing Company designs, reinforced by judicious additions to their number, and if the glamour of creating new designs had been forgone, results might have been better. The Committee on Types of Motive Power should have been empowered and directed to discharge its remit quickly – certainly by the end of 1948 – so that the proper decisions could be taken.

The Committee reported in October 1951. Its Chairman was J. L. Harrington, Chief Officer (Administration), who had been a valued aide of Missenden. The report was clear and well argued. Its main recommendations were: (1) diesel traction should be used for shunting at all appropriate locations; (2) a Great Northern Main Line electrification scheme should be developed immediately; (3) there should be a main-line trial diesel conversion scheme based on, notionally, the use of 100 locomotives of 2,000 hp; and (4) a scheme should be developed for the use of a fleet of modern diesel railcars.

The Committee recognised that: (a) steam would have to continue as 'an important element . . . for many years' but also that 'there is no prospect of removing its inherent limitations and disadvantages'; and (b) the Regions did have some electrification schemes mostly not of a main-line character either approved or in contemplation.

The report would have been timely had it

29. A curiosity: Ivatt D3 4–4–0 no. 2000, rebuilt with a North Eastern type of cab and retained for working Directors' and officers' specials, photographed running light on the up fast line through Essendine in June 1948, presumably to connect with the saloon somewhere nearby.

P. H. Wells

come three years earlier and had its recommendations been promptly implemented. As it was, the Executive ignored the 'guts' of the proposals, the GN main-line electrification and the major diesel main-line conversion scheme.

It would nevertheless be wrong to suggest that the Executive was entirely hostile to electric and diesel traction. It merely saw them as fulfilling a minor role for the foreseeable future. On electric traction, the Railway Executive had inherited from the companies two major electrification projects on the LNER, and a comprehensive programme for extending the Southern electrified network. Both of the LNER schemes were carried through to completion. The Liverpool Street–Shenfield electrification was opened in 1949. The Manchester–Sheffield/Wath scheme (the first main-line electrification involving a substantial freight traffic) was bound up with the construction of a new tunnel at Woodhead, at the summit of the line, and it was in fact not fully opened until 1954, just after the Executive had been abolished. The Eastern Region was already engaged on some preliminary planning for electrification of the suburban lines from Liverpool Street to Enfield, Chingford and Bishop's Stortford.

The Executive also set up one committee to consider the system of electrification and another to prepare a scheme for electrifying the London Tilbury and Southend line of the Eastern Region. This scheme was approved in principle by the Commission but had to wait until the 1955 Modernisation Plan before work on it could start.

30. Great Western enterprise: the gas turbine locomotive no. 18000, ordered before nationalisation, running in BR livery on a test run from Swindon, photographed on Reading West curve.

John Ashman FRPS

31. An ingenious experimental design which failed to survive; the Fell main-line diesel-mechanical locomotive no. 10100 ready to leave Derby for St Pancras on the London Midland Region.

W. Philip Conolly

The Southern Railway had, shortly before nationalisation, approved in principle the electrification of all the steam-operated main lines of that Company east of Reading and Portsmouth. The Executive kept this item on the agenda, but the scheme had to wait for the Modernisation Plan before work could start.

Shortly before the Executive's demise, it obtained BTC authority for extending the Liverpool Street–Shenfield electrification to Chelmsford and Southend. This actually was something of a victory for the Eastern Region. The London Tilbury and Southend electrification had been planned in outline by a 'headquarters committee'; this was resented in the Region, which set out to demonstrate that it would be better to give priority to extending to Southend (Victoria) the Shenfield scheme already in operation. The Executive conceded the point and saved face by announcing in the BTC Annual Report that 'this scheme is planned to come into operation before the line from Fenchurch Street to Southend (Central) is electrified, since it will provide not only a much improved service between Liverpool Street, Ilford, Romford, Chelmsford and Southend, but also an alternative route whilst major engineering works on the

3043
5

Fenchurch Street line are in hand as a preliminary to electrification'. A graceful retreat!

Towards the end of the period the Executive carried out experiments with 50 Hz, 25 kVa electric traction – the system eventually adopted for main-line electrification under the Modernisation Plan – by converting the small Lancaster–Heysham–Morecambe line on the London Midland Region, though actual operation only started a couple of months before the Executive's demise.

During the period 1945–53, under the 1935–40 New Works Programme which had been suspended during the war, BR were able to discard some steam suburban services in favour of London Transport. This programme had been supported by the Government as a means of alleviating unemployment. The former LNER branches to High Barnet, Alexandra Palace and Edgware were to be operated by London Transport Northern Line tube trains. The ex-LNER lines from Stratford to Loughton, Hainault and Ongar and the former Great Western services from Paddington as far as West Ruislip were to be operated by the Central Line.

Some of this work was completed just before nationalisation, but a decision hung fire over the projection of the Northern Line. This was eventually cut back, by an agreement between the Railway and London Transport Executives to abandon the sections from Highgate to Alexandra Palace, and from Mill Hill East to Edgware. Green Belt planning restrictions on development in the areas to be served were adduced as the main reason for these decisions, announced by London Transport in two stages between 1950 and 1953.

So far as diesel traction is concerned, the Executive had inherited from the former Companies several locomotive building projects, which, unlike the LNER East Coast diesel scheme, had progressed too far to be cancelled. From the LMS came the two English Electric 1,600 hp main-line passenger engines, delivered in 1949, and an 827 hp mixed-freight engine, delivered in 1950. The GWR had commissioned two gas-turbine-electric main-line locomotives, one from Switzerland and one from British builders. The Swiss unit started trials in 1950 and the British one in 1951. The Southern Railway had ordered three 1,600 hp main-line locomotives, which were delivered in 1950 and 1951. In addition, the Executive had on order a unique diesel-mechanical locomotive with the 4–8–4 wheel arrangement, employing a novel transmission invented by Lt-Col Fell.

Of these, the most successful were the LMS English Electric pair, Nos 10,000 and 10,001, which worked in service for some years. The least successful were the 'Fell' diesel-mechanical and the 827 hp type, which never performed for any length of time in revenue-earning service.

The last-named was the subject of a prolonged wrangle between the Executive and the contractors as to where the responsibility lay for its unsatisfactory performance. The Commission finally lost patience with the Executive and directed that the files be sent across for examination. I had the task of ploughing through the endless correspondence and reporting on where the mistakes appeared to have been made.

The gas-turbine locomotives originally

32 (*above*). Southern orthodox electric traction; 6-PUL set on a Sussex Coast express waiting to leave London Bridge station.

J. H. Aston

33 (*below*). Diesel main-line traction on the Southern; 1–Co–Co–1 diesel-electric locomotive no. 10201 with the 1 pm Waterloo to Plymouth express, passing under the flyover at Worting Junction, west of Basingstoke, on 8 September 1952.

Brian Morrison

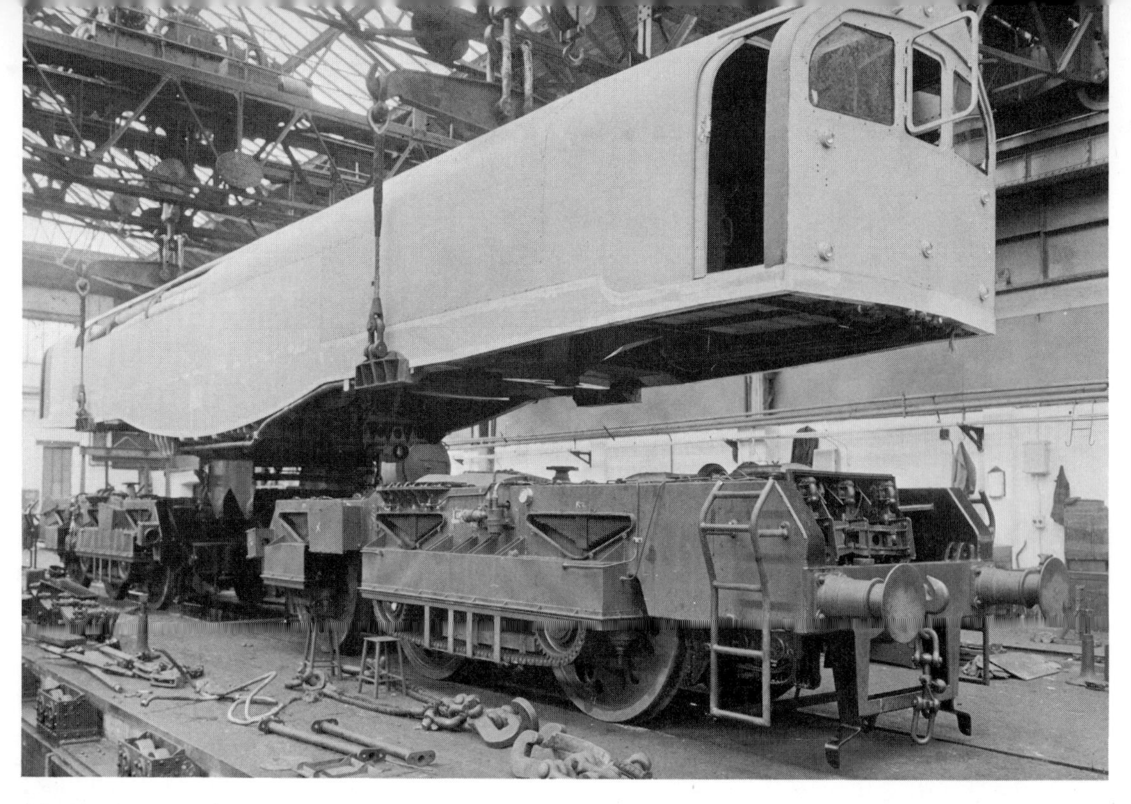

34. Southern unorthodoxy: the revolutionary Leader class prototype steam locomotive, designed by O. V. S. Bulleid, under construction at Brighton works. The unique chain drive can be clearly seen.

National Railway Museum

ordered by the GWR were also unsuccessful. But it is difficult to escape the conclusion that the trials of all these costly prototypes – some of which had potential that could have been developed in production units – were conducted sporadically and without any real interest in achieving success. On the contrary, the dedicated steam engineers seemed thankful when the tarpaulins could be thrown over the irritating diesel locos and they could be banished to some remote siding or corner of a workshop.

The diesel 'multiple-unit' concept, supplanting the original idea of 'railcars' or single self-propelled vehicles, had a less unhappy history. The Commission in 1951 was strengthened on the railway side by the appointment of F. A. Pope, who had been a Vice-President of the LMS before nationalisation and since then Chairman of the Ulster Transport Authority. His experiences in Northern Ireland had convinced him of the virtues of diesel units as a cheaper alternative to steam locomotives and conventional trains on lightly used branch and secondary services. He took a personal role in pressing the Railway Executive to move more effectively in this field.

The Executive (responding both to the

35. It did actually run! The Leader class locomotive no. 36001 on a test trip, Eastleigh to Woking, passing Allbrook signal box on 23 August 1950.

Les Elsey

36. The first BR Standard steam locomotive makes its bow: 4–6–0 mixed-traffic no. 73000 under close inspection at Marylebone station on 26 April 1951. Constructed at Derby, this was the first of a batch of thirty. Emphasis was laid on the design of the driver's cab in which the controls were all arranged so that the driver could reach them from a sitting position.

Keystone

37. BR Standard light-weight 4–6–0 mixed-traffic locomotive no. 75006 seen at Reading in September 1951, a few days after its completion. This class numbered eighty when building ceased in 1956.

P. J. Lynch

38. BR Standard class 4MT 2–6–4T no. 80013, showing the similarity with the LMS Stanier design of this type. It is seen arriving at East Croydon with an Oxted line train, composed mostly of SE&CR 'birdcage' stock, on 28 February 1953. No less than 155 engines of this class were built between 1951 and 1957.

pressure from the Commission spearheaded by Pope and to the recommendation of its own Committee on Types of Motive Power) did in fact appoint an oddly-named additional committee – the Light Weight Trains Committee – to study what could be done in this field. Proposals were put forward for several schemes, though none came into effect until after the Executive had been abolished.

Meanwhile the Commission had been exasperated to receive from the Executive a proposal to operate several local services with push-and-pull steam locomotives and carriage sets. This appeared to be a deliberate flouting of the Commission's wishes, as indeed did the standard steam locomotive building policy which continued, oblivious of the proposals of the Executive's own Committee on Types of Motive Power.

That programme had gained considerable momentum by the time that the Railway Executive was abolished in October 1953 and steam lost its principal champion with the retirement of R. A. Riddles. The British Transport Commission which absorbed into itself the functions of the Executive soon made it

39. Before the wires reached Southend: B 17/4 4–6–0 of LNER design, no. 61648, 'Arsenal', on a Liverpool Street–Southend train climbing the Brentwood bank on 9 May 1953.

Brian Morrison

40. The experimental a.c. 50-cycle high-voltage electrification of the Lancaster–Morecambe–Heysham section of the London Midland Region. A three-coach electric train is departing from Morecambe (Promenade) station for Heysham on 17 August 1953.

British Rail

clear that there must be a fresh look at traction policy and this was embodied in the Modernisation Plan of 1955, though by that time the new organisation had conferred so much power upon the Regions that a single, coherent traction policy for BR was wellnigh impossible.

Some people have nostalgia for the BR 'standard' steam locomotives as examples of the golden age of steam, prematurely displaced by less interesting forms of motive power. They are already represented by exhibits in the National Railway Museum at York. Others feel that, whatever part steam still had to play on British Railways in the 1950s and 1960s, it was putting the cart before the horse to commit such heavy resources to a design and construction programme for entirely new types before a long-term traction policy had been worked out and the remaining rôle for steam established.

It was this waste of precious time that produced the inevitable but rather regrettable reaction – the scramble to 'dieselise' under the later Modernisation Plan, and the rapid proliferation of types, far too many of which proved unsatisfactory. A steady, controlled programme of diesel development from 1948 to 1953 would have laid much better foundations for the future. Meanwhile steam could have been more gradually phased out, instead of being thrust on to the scrap-heap in a hurry whilst there were still many years of useful life in recently built locomotives.

6

The Carrying Stock

If the justification for building standard steam locomotives was questionable, the case for standardising carriage and wagon design was far stronger. Whatever the future form of traction, vehicles would be needed. Standardisation and long production runs should reduce manufacturing costs. The commercial appeal of really modern passenger coaches giving superior riding comfort would be immense.

In the diversity of passenger carriages inherited from the Companies there was scope for improvement and innovation. Each railway had had its strong points and weaknesses. Gresley had given the LNER his articulated stock – logical in concept, since resting the ends of adjacent carriages on a single bogie yielded economies in first cost; it also slightly reduced train lengths overall, which was specially useful in suburban train sets where the ratio of seats to overall length was an important economic factor. It was however doubtful whether the articulated sets – for example those in the high speed streamlined trains such as the 'Coronation' – rode quite as smoothly as Gresley's conventional main-line stock, which was outstandingly comfortable at high speed, largely due to his use of a heavy (and expensive) double bolster bogie.

Gresley had also introduced the 'Buckeye' centre coupling and buffer combined – superior in safety and in speed of coupling to the conventional screw coupling and side buffers, but inclined to produce jerks when trains started.

The achievements of the Great Western's distinguished locomotive engineers had not been fully matched in their coaching stock; that railway sported a surprising variety of designs, all solidly constructed but often very old-fashioned in style.

The Southern had acquired a reasonably modern fleet of locomotive-hauled carriages, stemming originally from the designs of Surrey Warner whom Walker had brought from the LSWR to join Maunsell. The main-line multiple-unit sets for the Brighton and Portsmouth electrifications had massive bodies but unfortunately the 'Eastleigh' bogie gave poor riding almost from the outset. Later electric stock produced under Bulleid's management was among the least attractive of its kind – hard riding and spartan internally.

I have left the LMS to the last. This railway had inherited a tradition of great excellence in carriage design, above all on the Midland where Clayton and Bain had established a great tradition of smooth riding and seating comfort.

Equally high standards applied to the best London & North Western stock designed by C. A. Park. The twelve-wheeled bogies of the Midland and LNWR dining-cars gave a superlative ride, as did the splendid 'Grampian' corridor stock of the Caledonian Railway.

The LMS, however, in pursuit of business efficiency, became over-obsessed with reducing the first cost of rolling stock. Its all-steel standard carriages, admittedly a good production engineering conception, suffered from the paring down of overall weight in the interests of economy and never rode quite as well as the best Midland or North Western carriages had done in their heyday.

41. Not universally approved! Exterior view of 'At the Sign of the Three Plovers', standing at Clapham Junction on 21 July 1951. The imitation brickwork and half-timbering painted on the exterior panelling, which caused so much criticism, can be seen.

H. C. Casserley

42. Pullman luxury of the traditional type. Class A1 Pacific no. 60158, then un-named, leaving King's Cross with the down 'Tees-Tyne Pullman' on 2 May 1951. The 'Hadrian Bar' contained kitchen and a cocktail bar for passengers.

P. J. Lynch

43. Another tavern car: the fake 'Old English Tavern' interior of one of the restaurant-buffet cars introduced in May 1949 on the Eastern and Southern Regions. The car illustrated had an inn sign, 'The Jolly Tar', and was on show at Waterloo station. Note the New Look costumes of the lady customers.

Keystone

is now, and can be for some time to come, only a limited scope for their use'. Discussions about extending their use were pursued with the National Coal Board and major coal consumers. But it was not until 1953 that production got under way, and in that year – the year of the Executive's demise – 650 were built.

In the six years of the Executive's life some progress was undoubtedly made towards standardisation. At the outset there had been 480 different types of wagon in stock and the Executive's initial proposal had been to reduce this number to 150. Sweeping condemnation and scrapping of the former private owners' wagons – largely grease-lubricated – which had been acquired for British Railways on nationalisation demanded, it was thought, substantial new construction.

But the total wagon stock at vesting day (excluding service vehicles) was just under 1,224,000. Could a fleet of this size be needed under unified operation and ownership? Was not even 150 types excessive?

If the age-distribution of the wagon fleet had been reasonably even, and if thirty-five years is accepted as a normal book life, replacements of the order of 35,000 a year would have been needed. Actual construction (excluding service vehicles) was as follows:

1948	39,000
1949	32,000
1950	28,000
1951	37,000
1952	28,000
1953	41,000

This, averaged over the six years, is close enough to the theoretical norm. But with hindsight one can see that it was out of line with the trend of traffic after 1955; and, with improved systems of wagon control, even in the 1950s a much smaller fleet could have been envisaged.

The good intentions of the early days in regard to continuous brakes, advanced forms of coupling and so forth had produced little by the end of the Executive's lifetime. It was left for the BTC in the Modernisation Plan of 1955 to reactivate interest in these developments.

The small four-wheeled wagon, often equipped only with loose couplings and without continuous brakes, survived and with the changeover to diesel traction became an embarrassment owing to its propensity to derail itself at speed. It was the need to eliminate this distressing characteristic which produced the fundamental research at the Derby Research Centre into the behaviour of wheels, axles and suspension systems that, in the 1970s, led to the concept of the Advanced Passenger Train and the long-wheelbase high capacity wagon that BR are at last building to replace the obsolete wagon fleet that is largely a legacy of the early years after nationalisation.

7

Accidents and Incidents

In the first year after nationalisation an unlikely incident occurred in an unlikely month. On 12 and 13 August 1948 there were unprecedented floods in Northumberland and south-east Scotland. The East Coast Main Line was broken by the complete demolition of seven bridges, whilst there were also landslides and subsidences leaving the track suspended in the air at several places. The track as far north as Tweedmouth was restored in a couple of days, but between Berwick and Edinburgh the repairs involved using military-type bridging material and substantial earthwork restoration.

Trains were diverted from Tweedmouth over the cross-country line (quite unsuitable for fast running) of the former North Eastern Railway as far as Kelso where former North British metals were reached and the Waverley route to Edinburgh was joined at St Boswells.

Floods of this magnitude had been quite unknown in Britain, and the reconstruction on a permanent basis of all the broken bridges was a huge task. Meanwhile travellers between England and Scotland were able to appreciate some unfamiliar areas of border scenery until 1 November when the East Coast Main Line was reopened.

The year was also marked by three major accidents on the London Midland Region. The first serious accident was at Winsford, north of Crewe, on 17 April, when the Glasgow–Euston train had been stopped by a passenger pulling the communication cord – allegedly because a soldier wanted to get off at Winsford station, near his home. The stationary train was run into by the following 'Postal' from Glasgow because the signalman erroneously assumed that the earlier train had passed his box and he then cleared the road for the 'Postal'. The impact took place at about 45 mph and sixteen lives were lost in the last two coaches of the stationary train.

Not long afterwards came the second accident on the London Midland Region, at Wath Road on 18 May. This was a derailment of the 11.45 am express from St Pancras to Bradford when travelling along an embankment at 60–65 mph. Seven passengers died; the cause was established at the Ministry of Transport inquiry as being distortion of the track due to expansion of the rails in the very hot weather.

At the height of the summer the Eastern Region also suffered a derailment on 17 July, when in the early morning the 7.50 pm Edinburgh to King's Cross, headed by A2/1 Pacific, 'Duke of Rothesay', came off the track as it emerged from the New Southgate tunnel.

Later that same day, at 5.8 pm in the Scottish Region, the 3.30 pm express from Aberdeen to Glasgow collided at Ardler Junction with the 4.20 pm train from Dundee West to Blairgowrie. This was a converging collision caused by the driver of the branch-line train having wrongly read a signal and passed it at danger as he approached the junction. Whilst three train crew members were killed on this unlucky day, there were no passenger fatalities in either accident.

But bad luck still dogged the London Midland Region. On 30 November an unusual accident took place at Stockport in dense fog and darkness. Two trains from Manchester to Buxton had been combined and formed with two locomotives; in the fog the drivers, whilst the train was standing at Heaton Norris station, mistook a verbal message as implying that the starting signal (which they could not see) had cleared. They started the train and ran into the back of another train, from Manchester to Crewe and Disley (also combined and double-headed), which was stationary on the

48. The East Coast floods of 1948. The temporary bridge, no. 133, replacing the one over the Eye Water, between Berwick and Dunbar, which was swept away by the storm water. A test load is standing on the bridge prior to reopening the line to traffic.

National Railway Museum

49. The Harrow accident of 8 October 1952: a picture that tells its own story only too clearly.

Keystone

track, waiting for signals. Two coaches of the stationary train were telescoped even though the speed of the colliding train was put at no more than 10–15 mph; five passengers were killed and five seriously injured.

1949 was, by contrast, a fortunate year – not a single passenger was killed in a train accident, the best record for any year since 1908.

But in 1950 the bad luck of the London Midland Region reappeared. On 27 August, at about 3 am, the up 'Irish Mail' from Holyhead collided at Penmaenmawr with a light engine which had been making a shunting movement in the station. The collision took place at between 60 and 70 mph and there was much damage. Five passengers and a sleeping-car attendant died, according to the Inspecting Officer's report because of failures to follow the rules by the signalman, the driver of the light engine, and a guard travelling with him.

An unusual series of fires occurred on express passenger trains between 1949 and 1951: one at Penmanshiel between Berwick and Edinburgh on 23 June 1949; one at Beattock on 8 June 1950; and one at Huntingdon on 14 July 1951. In the first, one passenger was injured, and in the last twenty-two received burns or cuts; unhappily five died in the Beattock disaster.

Great concern was felt at these fires and the

causes were investigated in detail. The design of the carriages was criticised in that a cigarette end or a lighted match thrown down could have set fire to accumulated dust and rubbish in the Beattock disaster. But in the ex-LNER coaches involved in the Penmanshiel and Huntingdon fires, it was the use of nitro-cellulose lacquer, highly inflammable, as a covering for interior partitions that was found to be responsible. All the coaches that had been so treated were withdrawn from service for modification.

1951 was a bad year – the British Transport Commission for the first time referred in their Annual Report to the accidents that had taken place involving forty-four passenger deaths. The first serious accident was at Doncaster on 16 March: an express from Doncaster to King's Cross was derailed at a speed of 20–25 mph passing over a scissors crossover; coaches slewed broadside against a bridge and were crushed. There were fourteen passenger deaths – surprising in an accident at such a relatively low speed.

This was followed by a rear-end collision at Ford on the Southern Region on 5 August, when an electric train from Brighton to Portsmouth collided with another train, having overrun a signal. Again, although the speed of the collision was low, about 18 mph, there were serious casualties, eight passengers killed and forty-seven injured.

Electric trains were also involved in the accident a fortnight later at Newcastle Central on the North Eastern Region. On 17 August an electric train left a platform, against the starting-signal which was at danger, and collided with another train that was entering the adjacent platform under a clear sign. Two passengers died in consequence. The cause was assumed to be that the driver of the departing train (who was killed) had started on receiving the guard's notification that the train was ready to go, without checking that the signal was 'off'.

This accident was followed by another on 21 September at Weedon on the London Midland Region when the 8.20 Liverpool to Euston express left the rails at 60–65 mph. The engine fell down a twelve-foot embankment and there was severe damage to the leading coaches, in which passengers and a dining-car attendant were fatally injured. The cause was established as bad maintenance of the leading bogie on the Pacific locomotive, allowing a wheel to mount the rail.

The last accident of consequence during the year, in which happily no one was killed and only two passengers were injured, was also a derailment on the London Midland Region. The 10.30 am Glasgow–Euston express left the rails at Polesworth owing to excessive speed over a crossover from the fast to the slow line – about 55 mph. The driver had missed the signal.

The following year, 1952, was marked by the worst disaster for very many years, the appalling accident at Harrow and Wealdstone, London Midland Region, on 8 October, in which 108 passengers lost their lives. At 8.18 am the sleeping car express from Perth ran into the rear of a local train, the 7.31 am from Tring to Euston, just as the latter was leaving the station. The wreckage was thrown across the down fast line and (as bad luck would have it) before the signalman could stop traffic on that line the 8 am express from Euston to Liverpool and Manchester, double-headed, ran into the debris. The whole station – all six tracks of the main line – was blocked by the carriages strewn across the line.

The cause of this terrible disaster, the worst since the 1915 Quintinshill collision on the Caledonian Railway, was overrunning of signals – distant, outer home and inner home – by the

8
4082

50. King George VI's funeral train at Paddington station, awaiting departure for Windsor, 15 February 1952. The locomotive, with the draped plaques of the Royal Coat of Arms on either side of the smoke-box, bears the nameplates, 'Windsor Castle'. It is not in fact that locomotive (which hauled the funeral train of King George V in 1936) but no. 7013, 'Bristol Castle'. The original 'Windsor Castle' locomotive was in Swindon works for overhaul at the time.

British Rail

driver of the train from Perth.

The other accident of note in that year was the derailment on 18 April at Blea Moor of the 9.15 'Thames–Clyde' express, from Glasgow to St Pancras, double-headed, at about 55 mph. The engines became derailed at facing points leading to the up loop line and there was considerable damage to the coaches, though fortunately nobody was killed. The Inspecting Officer's report criticised the maintenance of the leading locomotive, on which a tender brake rod had come adrift, struck the points and caused the derailment.

The other incident that should be recorded for this year is the provision of funeral trains when King George VI died at Sandringham on 6 February. Royal Trains conveying the body ran from Wolferton to King's Cross for the lying in state, and subsequently from Paddington to Windsor for the funeral.

In 1953 two very unusual disasters took place. On 31 January the BR car carrier vessel *Princess Victoria* was sunk by heavy seas whilst on passage from Stranraer to Larne. The weather conditions were described as 'approaching the limits of experience' at the time. The immediate cause of the ship's foundering was a huge sea that smashed through the car doors at the stern of the vessel, and the inadequacy of the freeing ports to dispose quickly of this huge weight of water. The total loss of life was 133. The radio officer of the *Princess Victoria* was posthumously awarded the George Cross for bravery. Subsequently the design of all car carriers was revised to eliminate the structural defects that had led to this disaster – one unparalleled, since railway ships had a high record of safety.

Strangely enough, little more than three months passed before another British Railways ship was in trouble. In May the *Duke of York*, on passage from Harwich to the Hook of Holland, was in collision, thirty-five miles east of Harwich, with a vessel owned by the USA Department of Commerce. Several lives were lost. This incident led to prolonged litigation over the responsibility for the collision.

There were also three railway accidents that should be recorded in the year, up to the date of the Railway Executive's demise. All took place in the late summer. On 8 August there was a derailment at Abington in the Scottish Region, near Beattock. The down 'Royal Scot' express was derailed owing to distortion of the track; heat had caused the rails to expand and buckle. Fortunately there were no fatalities or serious injuries.

A much more serious accident occurred on 15 August at Manchester, when a steam passenger train from Manchester to Bacup, passing over the Irk Valley Viaduct, came into sidelong contact with an electric train from Bury to Manchester. The first vehicle of the electric train fell into the river some thirty or forty feet below. There were ten fatalities and fifty-eight were injured. The Inspecting Officer's report placed the blame on the motorman of the electric train, who ran past the home signal at danger, and also on the signalman who allowed the steam train to cross the junction in violation of regulations.

This was followed on 18 September by a buffer-stop collision on the Southern Region at Guildford. An electric train from Waterloo to Guildford lost braking power whilst entering the terminal bay at Guildford and crashed through the buffers and into the stationmaster's office. The assistant stationmaster was killed; four railway staff and two passengers were injured.

Can any general conclusions be drawn from this record? It is unsafe to make sweeping statements about railway safety based on a few years' accident statistics. Chance, particularly in the form of human error, plays too large a part. But, looking over the record for the first six years after nationalisation, one has the feeling that there were too many train accidents that could have been prevented by the wider adoption of signalling technology of a kind that was available at the date in question.

The three main safeguards were: track circuiting, to help ensure that the signals display the correct aspect; colour-light signals in place of semaphores, to reduce the risk of drivers missing a signal through inattention or poor visibility; and automatic train control, to ensure that a driver passing an adverse signal is audibly warned and that the train is stopped if the warning is ignored.

The Inspecting Officers of Railways, in reports upon individual accidents and also in their Annual Reports, regularly drew attention to cases in which one or other of these improvements would have mitigated or prevented disaster. They particularly stressed the advantage conferred by automatic train control (ATC).

Sir Cyril Hurcomb, Chairman of the BTC, was mindful of the Commission's duty under Section 3(1) of the 1947 Act to have 'due regard to safety of operation'. He wanted to ensure that the Commission had a full answer to any critics, and – in a favourite phrase – he insisted that there must be 'a policy, a plan and a programme'.

In the event, a lot of dragging of feet went on. The Commission was alarmed at the estimates of cost involved and agreed to hasten slowly. And the Railway Executive had some excuse for delay. There were two ATC systems in existence – the GWR one, based on physical contact between a shoe on the locomotive and a ramp between the rails, installed on all the main lines of the Western Region; and an LMS system, only installed on a relatively short stretch of line, employing a magnetic, non-contact design. The GWR system was robust and simple, and had been widely tested in service. It was not perfect – a rough-riding locomotive bouncing on its springs might, very occasionally, fail to get the audible signal –

51. British Railways Automatic Warning System; a close-up view of the engine receiver passing over track inductors. The locomotive is A4 Pacific 'Sir Nigel Gresley'.

British Rail

52. The ill-fated ss *Princess Victoria*, built in 1947 for the Stranraer–Larne car ferry service, which foundered on passage in a storm described as 'approaching the limits of experience'.

British Rail

though, even so, it was a marked advance on having absolutely nothing to back up the visual signals. The LMS system was rather more complicated and had not been so widely tested in use. The Executive felt, not unreasonably, that it could evolve a BR design incorporating the best features of the two existing systems. This process took a long time – many people thought too long.

There was also a conflict of views within the Executive. Some operators – especially on the Southern Region, which had the greatest mileage of colour-light signalling and the highest traffic density – argued that a considerably greater contribution to safety could be obtained for any given investment, if the money were laid out on replacing semaphores by colour-light signals and with continuous track circuiting.

In the Annual Report for 1949 the Executive announced that it was making trials with a 'warning control' device (based on a modification of the LMS system) on the down East Coast Main Line between New Barnet and Huntingdon, a distance of fifty single-track miles. But it warned that restrictions on capital investment would delay the execution of any programme for speeding up the installation of safety devices. Thereafter it lapsed into silence for a long time. At last, in the 1952 Annual Report it was announced that what appeared to be a satisfactory prototype for a BR system had been evolved. During 1953 some fifty-four locomotives were equipped with the apparatus so that extended trials could be carried out, but it was not until the Modernisation Plan of 1955 that the Commission were able to announce that a sum of £20 million had been earmarked for the progressive introduction of ATC – soon to become redesignated as AWS, the Automatic Warning System.

8

The Rank and File

It is difficult, after such a lapse of time, to analyse exactly why most railwaymen in the wages grades, and many in the salaried grades, supported nationalisation – at any rate before it happened. Trade unionists naturally backed the Labour Party's election programme. Individuals probably expected that wages and working conditions would be improved and that some form of worker participation in management, or industrial democracy, would appear. A few who had foreign contacts, or who had been able to inform themselves about conditions on the Continent, considered that railwaymen in the State railways of European countries enjoyed pensions and also pay and status superior to those of their British counterparts under private enterprise.

But following vesting day worker participation was scarcely visible, except that two former trade union general secretaries had been appointed to membership of the Transport Commission and the Railway Executive respectively. Otherwise the bosses seemed to have changed little. After a time, the desire of the Executive to standardise practices throughout BR led to a succession of directives and changes in established practice which, human nature being what it is, were more often met with irritation or even derision than welcomed as evidence of the millennium having arrived.

The Commission, as the paymaster, had the last word in negotiations over pay, although the Executive was in the forefront as being, under the Act, the actual employer. The Commission's Chairman entrusted labour relations to John (later Sir John) Benstead. It soon became apparent that his trade union background had not made him a weak negotiator on management's side of the table; on the contrary, he was not disposed to be generous with the Commission's money and was a tough nut to crack in every way.

But for the first few years inflation was not yet exerting the irresistible pressure on railway wage rates that it did later; in fact, the main problem was recruitment to fill vacancies – recruitment, that is, of suitable staff who would develop into railwaymen of calibre equal to those of the pre-war period. Some unsuitable individuals were recruited whom the older and more traditional railwaymen regarded with disfavour. It was becoming impossible to fill the starting grades with school leavers whose first job might be engine cleaner when better paid and less arduous work was offered at local factories.

As early as 1948, however, the Commission did set up machinery for joint consultation which they described in their Annual Report for that year as 'the means of liaison at the highest level between the Commission and the Executive and the representatives of the staff'. The good intentions were there; and, in another field, that of welfare, the Railway Executive in the same year established a Joint Advisory Council for Welfare to deal with matters such as 'amenities in workshops, offices and canteens, messrooms and hostels, hygienic facilities, the welfare of women and junior staff, social and recreational facilities, accident prevention and first aid'.

These measures were of course entirely outside the machinery of negotiation on pay and conditions of work, for which an elaborate procedure existed, developed from the original Conciliation Scheme sponsored by Lloyd George, at that time President of the Board of Trade, as long ago as 1906.

The first shots in the campaign to improve wages were fired by the NUR (National Union of Railwaymen), who made a claim for a flat increase of 12s 6d (62½p) a week for all grades in August 1948. This was rejected. In May 1949 the NUR put in a claim for a flat 10s (50p) a week plus more pay for Saturday afternoons and evenings. This too was rejected and on Ministry intervention was referred to a Government-appointed special Board of Conciliation. That Board turned down the basic NUR demands but recommended some minor concessions.

By early 1950 things were hotting up. The NUR asked for a minimum wage of £5 for all railwaymen and they were joined by the other two unions – ASLEF and the RCA (Railway Clerks Association, later renamed the Transport Salaried Staffs' Association). The claim was rejected, but some minor concessions were again made.

In August 1950 demands came in from all three Unions – from the NUR for a 10 per cent rise all round, from ASLEF for a 15 per cent rise, and from the RCA for a 7½ per cent rise. No agreement being reached, a Ministry of Labour Court of Inquiry was set up. After much argument a settlement at about 7½ per cent was reached.

By early August 1951 – the holiday season apparently being regarded as a favourable one for lodging claims – another round of demands, mainly for a 10 per cent increase, was made. Settlement – reached this time through the normal negotiating machinery – was on the basis of 8 per cent plus some minor concessions. The Unions promptly deposited new claims which were finally settled in November 1952, again at a lower level than the claim, and again through the normal machinery of negotiation.

Every year the Commission dolefully recorded in their Annual Report the cost of meeting these pay claims but refrained from commenting upon them. They gave no hint as to whether they considered that the claims were justified – in other words, whether the management were getting value for money – or whether they felt they were being forced into paying too much. Productivity – apart from pious generalisations – was not being discussed very realistically at this stage.

By 1953 the usual round of summer demands had arrived. The increases claimed were substantial, in many cases up to 15 per cent. They were referred to the conciliation machinery where much smaller increases were awarded. The NUR then threatened to strike just before Christmas. A last-minute agreement was reached, under which the award would be implemented immediately and a further improvement would be made at a later date.

Another good intention was declared: that the Commission 'would examine with the Unions the whole wage and salary structure

53. The School of Transport established by the LMS Railway at Derby contained an elaborate model railway lay-out upon which operating practices and problems were demonstrated by instructors. Here a train is being signalled onto a single line section; the man on the right is holding the tablet which the driver would require as an authority to enter the section.

British Rail

and that the Unions would confer in order to evolve ways of increasing the efficiency of the railway organisation'. But by this time the Railway Executive had been abolished and the Commission had taken over the management of the railways.

During the six years of the Executive's existence staff numbers had not fallen much. There are many pitfalls in using statistics as an index of productivity, but the following figures are an indication of only a modest improvement in productivity in a situation where traffic was changing relatively little.

One must ask whether staff policy had been

	1948	1949	1950	1951	1952	1953
BR staff (including railway road haulage) (thousands)	649	625	605	600	601	594
Index (1948 = 100) of staff	100	96·3	93·2	92·4	92·6	91·5
Index of originating tons of freight	100	101·4	101·8	103·3	103·3	104·7
Index of passenger journeys	100	99·7	98·6	100·5	99·3	98·9

as effective and enlightened as it should have been. It is difficult to avoid the conclusion that it showed very little advance on the policies and tactics that the former Companies had followed before nationalisation. A major example is the question of pensions for wages grade staff. These had not existed under company management, although there had been sectional schemes sponsored by the staff themselves. As a matter of social justice, and as a valuable means of attracting responsible staff intending to make their careers with the railway, there was a gap that ought to be filled under nationalisation. In their first Annual Report the Commission declared their intention of looking at this; but progress was desperately slow – at times imperceptible. It was not until August 1967 that a wages grade pension scheme – on lines that could hardly be considered generous – was finally launched, nearly twenty years after nationalisation.

Many people commented upon the differences in fringe benefits enjoyed by the British railwayman and his French or German counterparts. Housing assistance, medical services, holiday quarters and pensions – in all these the Continental was better off. No doubt this contributed substantially to improving the morale and in many cases the performance of men who valued their employment and the privileges it conferred.

The British tradition of voluntary or charitable effort in such matters had produced bodies such as the Railway Benevolent Institution and the Railway Convalescent Homes, as well as individual 'sick clubs' and other welfare organisations; but there was no comprehensive and centrally financed system of social security – nor did one appear under nationalisation.

Recruitment and training was another field in which the railways were woefully weak. The old tradition that any vacancy could be filled by a youngster keen to join the railway service was killed during the war, yet both the Companies before nationalisation and the Railway Executive after it failed to update their procedures. Vacancies were merely notified to the local labour exchange and the adult recruits who appeared were all too often those whom other industries, paying higher wages, did not want. A great opportunity was lost in the early years of British Railways. Direct recruitment centres, staffed by professionally trained interviewers, should have been set up and the labour exchanges need not have been used.

Training is the counterpart to recruitment: it is no use recruiting scientifically if the recruit is not thereafter properly inducted into his work and equipped to perform it. Here the Executive inherited relatively little from the Companies. There were some signalling schools and Enginemen's Mutual Improvement Classes were held at various centres. There was a patchwork of courses in particular subjects, mostly organised locally, but concentrated on the LNER at the All-Line Commercial and Operating Schools at Faverdale and Darlington, and on the Southern at the Woking Training School, which in 1959 was transformed into the British Transport Staff College. The LMS had built at Derby a residential School of Transport which provided vocational courses in subjects such as railway operating. But these facilities in total were quite inadequate to establish the desirable general principle that every recruit to the railway service, in the traffic grades at any rate, should start work only after he had undergone an appropriate training course and passed a proficiency test. Much damage was done to the railway public image by allowing raw recruits, not even equipped with a uniform but merely sporting an armband, to be thrown in contact with the public.

Management training was a different story. The LNER had inherited from the former North Eastern Railway a system of recruiting university graduates and giving them, together with a selected number of promising young men on the staff, a three-year training period as 'traffic apprentices', in the course of which they were given an insight into the working of all the main railway departments. This was a valuable way of spotting and encouraging future managerial talent, and it helped to overcome the rigid departmentalisation that was a long-standing defect of the railway organisation. Its results had been very satisfactory to the LNER board who always patriotically argued that the intellectual level of that railway's manager class was the highest in the Big Four.

The LNER scheme had been imitated, with rather less energy and conviction, by the other three Companies before the war. On nationalisation, it was adopted by the Railway Executive in very much its LNER form for British Railways as a whole.

But this was the glamour end of the training function. The serious deficiencies in recruitment and training methods, and the traditional concentration of the BR staff department upon the quantity of labour costs, rather than the quality of the labour output, continued. It was based upon an elaborate ritual which seemed to appeal to BR officers and union negotiators – both skilled in procedural niceties – whereby the moves, as in chess, of claim followed by rejection followed by appeal followed by compromise, were understood and even enjoyed by both sides as tests of individual skill and toughness. Whether in the long run the business benefited is more doubtful. A more positive and imaginative approach to wage negotiations, linking these with productivity, had to wait for more than a decade after the Railway Executive had disappeared.

9

Ships and Sealing Wax

The Railway Companies owned many businesses besides railway systems – ships, ports, hotels, canals, workshops. They had investments in bus companies, in road haulage, travel agencies and air transport. Nationalisation involved a considerable re-shuffling of activities. Some – at any rate for the time being – were left in the hands of the Railway Executive. These included the ships, the packet ports, the workshops, property management, and road collection and delivery vehicles. But, in pursuit of tidy administration, under the Transport Act, 1947 some activities were taken away and placed under other Executives whilst others came under the direct control of the Commission.

To part of this The Railway Executive did not object. It handed over the railway-owned canals to the Docks and Inland Waterways Executive without any regrets. It accepted the necessity of handing over the South Wales, Humber and Scottish railway-owned ports to the same Executive, though this involved difficult problems of drawing boundaries between 'railway' and 'docks' assets; as a consequence some transfers were delayed for a while. The Railway Executive fought hard to retain Southampton, but lost and the handover took place on 1 September 1950.

Also with regret but no resistance, the railway hotels – as well as station and train catering – were handed over to the Hotels Executive set up on 7 June 1948.

The investments in bus companies were a problem. The railway shareholdings had entitled the Companies to nominate directors of bus company boards; this was seen as a practical form of road–rail co-ordination. But the Commission had acquired the Tilling Group in November 1948 and the principle of compartmenting activities suggested a concentration of all the bus interests. For a time, however, the Railway Executive continued to nominate railway officers as directors on bus company boards.

The investment in road haulage firms – including the famous names of Carter Paterson and Pickfords, controlled through the railway ownership of Hay's Wharf Cartage Co. Ltd – had to be handed over to the new Road Transport Executive, which became the Road Haulage Executive in June 1949.

The Commission took direct control of some other former railway assets, such as the shares of Thomas Cook & Son Ltd, which had been jointly owned by the four Railway Companies, and also Dean and Dawson, the much smaller travel agency formerly owned

54. The ss *Brighton*, built for the Newhaven–Dieppe service, leaving Newhaven on 22 September 1952.

British Rail

by the LNER. It also took over the nominal ownership of Railway Air Services Ltd, which was never allowed to re-start operations after the war by a Government dedicated to the principle of assigning exclusive functions to monopolistic or semi-monopolistic public corporations.

The Commission felt that establishment of common services for the Executives should be logical and economical. The process started with the institution of a common legal service in January 1950. All the Executives would have preferred to keep their own legal services. The Railway and London Transport Executives argued their case for this hotly but they eventually had to give way.

Commercial advertising was the next to be wrenched away. It was set up as a central agency in March 1949. Other central activities created by the BTC were the Traffic Costing Service, and the Charges Division set up to work towards the preparation of charges schemes – applying in theory to the 'integrated' transport system envisaged by the Labour Government – for all the Executives.

The Railway Executive would have liked to carry on as the direct heir of the Railway Companies and to retain all the Company-owned business, except perhaps the canals. But it was clear that this was impossible. A lot of views had been expressed on whether the Railway Companies ought to have other interests than simply running the railway, since diversification is a source of strength to many businesses.

The intensity of road competition between the wars had made it obviously sensible to take a financial interest in road transport. In fact, the railways had been early investors in this field, and had operated their own bus services, without statutory powers, in various parts of the country even before the 1914–18 war, usually in connection with train services.

Again, the railway hotel business had started as an essential adjunct to rail travel, much as the inn proprietors and the stage-coach services had been associated many years ago. The canals were rather different; some had been bought up to stifle their opposition to railway Bills in Parliament, others to reduce competition or even in order that the railways could use their land for rail tracks. There was little interest on the part of the Companies in their canals; money for their maintenance was grudged and only provided insofar as there was a statutory obligation to do so.

Shipping services and the associated port facilities they required could on the other hand be regarded simply as projections of the train service, and it was logical for the railway Companies to operate them.

The railways had also built and managed workshops for not merely the repair but also the construction of locomotives, carriages and wagons, from the earliest days – in contrast with the practice in most other countries where private firms normally built all the locomotives and rolling stock for the railways. In Britain contractors merely supplied those items the railways were unable to obtain from their own workshops for any reason.

The Railway Companies had defended using the shareholders' money in this way to become in effect transport 'conglomerates' and equipment manufacturers, not just providers of rail transport. The opposite point of view was held by some civil servants and Labour politicians, who argued that widely dispersed interests weakened concentration and efficiency. It was said that in the nationalised sector the functions should be prescribed quite strictly and remits given to public corporations should not encourage or even permit of diversification.

This argument has in fact continued right up to the present day. The Railway Executive was able in its lifetime to hang on to the ships and packet ports, the railway workshops, the property business and the road collection and delivery fleets. All have since been detached and put under separate management boards under the British Railways Board, with the exception of the road vehicles which are now not under railway control at all, since National Carriers Ltd is a part of the National Freight Corporation's empire.

In the years under review, how did these 'ancillary businesses' fare? The Railway Executive was anxious to strengthen the shipping fleets, which had been depleted during the war. From the railway fleets no less than 92 ships out of the total of 130 were chartered by the Government at various stages of the war and many had been lost through enemy action. The Executive inherited projects from the Companies and in 1949 formulated a five-year building programme designed to meet expected traffic expansion and to replace wartime losses and life-expired vessels. The programme included thirteen cross-Channel and fourteen coastal waters and lake vessels.

In 1949 the MV *Hibernia*, the MV *Cambria* and the SS *Maid of Orleans* were added to the fleet; in 1950 came the SS *Amsterdam* for the Harwich–Hook of Holland service and the SS *Brighton* for the Newhaven–Dieppe route.

Next year came the MV *Norfolk Ferry* for the Harwich–Zeebrugge train ferry and three smaller vessels for estuarial routes; and in 1952 came the SS *Lord Warden* (the largest car carrier that had so far been built for the narrow seas), and the SS *Normannia* for the Southampton–Havre service.

The ships operated by the Railway Executive made a substantial contribution to the Commission's central charges and interest burdens. The net traffic receipts were as follows:

	£ million
1948	2·94
1949	3·11
1950	2·85
1951	2·88
1952	1·89
1953	0·95

The sharp fall in 1953 was due to a combination of a slight fall in traffic, a rise in wage rates and the costs of accident damage and compensation claims arising out of the accidents to the *Princess Victoria* and the *Duke of York*, mentioned in Chapter 7. (The results were somewhat better in the following year.)

In the railway workshops, an immediately beneficial effect was felt from matching needs and resources for the system as a whole. Even though the shops remained under Regional management, almost at once work began to be distributed to wherever there was spare capacity. As early as 1948 the workshops of the London Midland Region were repairing locomotives for the Western Region and components for other Regions were being manufactured in Western, Southern, Eastern and North Eastern Region shops.

The steam locomotive testing station at Rugby, planned before the war as a joint effort by the LMS and LNER, was completed and came into use at the end of 1948, though its useful life was, sadly, to be shortened abruptly by the decision to replace steam by diesel and electric traction only seven years later.

The Executive had lost, together with the hotels, control over train and station catering – the restaurant cars and refreshment rooms. These, unlike the hotels, were closely integrated into the railway's operations. Problems of demarcation and ownership had to be settled even though the former railway managerial staff continued working under the new Executive.

From the outset the Hotels Executive emphasised that the hotels constituted an independent business. There was some justification for arguing that railway travellers no longer provided the great majority of visitors. The Executive was eager to put its chain of hotels in the top international class, following a tradition of the former Midland Railway carried on under the LMS rather than to cater for the needs of the average traveller. The latter had been closer to the aims of the LNER, which maintained comfortable but unpretentious establishments in cities such as Bradford, Sheffield, Leeds, Peterborough and Hull which contrasted with the more expensive former LMS hotels in Manchester, Birmingham and Liverpool. The differences however were not always consistent; the LNER hotels in York and Edinburgh were the leading ones in those cities, for instance. The severing of the links between the railway and the hotels was a gradual business; at local level, the hotel managers and the railway officers often maintained an excellent relationship.

The Hotels Executive, however, was anxious to improve the finances of the restaurant cars. In the first year after nationalisation these showed a loss of £83,000, although the refreshment rooms had earned a profit of £435,000.

55. The ss *Amsterdam*, built by John Brown & Co, running her trials on the Clyde in May 1950 prior to entering the nightly Harwich (Parkeston Quay)–Hook of Holland service.

British Rail

Railwaymen might argue that catering on trains was an essential component of the passenger business, and that a loss on train catering might be justified by the fare receipts. But now that the money flowed into two quite separate pockets, cross-subsidisation would be ruled out. There was no question of the Railway Executive agreeing to fund losses on the restaurant cars in, for example, the way in which the Atchison Topeka and Santa Fé Railroad in the USA funded Fred Harvey, the catering contractor whose meals were of such excellence as to attract substantial numbers of passengers to the railway from competing lines.

The railway Companies had adopted different catering policies. Most of them ran the restaurant cars and refreshment rooms themselves, but the Southern had inherited a tradition of using outside catering firms – first Spiers & Pond, and later Frederick Hotels – on the south-western side, whilst the Pullman Car Company was the contractor on the Brighton and South-Eastern sides. Pullman services were also widespread on the LNER.

The reinstatement of the Pullman services (and in some cases their extension) has been recorded in Chapter 4. But the railway restaurant car services never recovered completely from the effects of wartime rationing, and the loss of experienced staff, during the lifetime of the Railway Executive.

The Hotels Executive's working surpluses (or deficits) over the period were:

	Hotels	Refreshment rooms	Restaurant cars
	£000	£000	£000
1948	103·6	435·6	– 83·5
1949	– 47·0	327·2	–514·2
1950	–190·7	222·5	–644·4
1951	34·6	329·0	–636·5
1952	42·4	315·4	–471·8
1953	– 11·1	189·6	–648·7

Perhaps it was small wonder that policy at times seemed to flounder in a desperate search for more receipts and reduced working costs. There were always critics who felt that an experienced and successful catering combine could have contrived to give better service and still make money. After all, Pullman did it. But the National Union of Railwaymen was then, as always, bitterly opposed to the principle of contracting out any operations that could be conducted by members of the union, even where (as in the case of Pullman) the working conditions and rates of pay were the subject of agreement with the union.

10 The End of the Beginning

Two events took place in 1952 that marked the end of what may be called the 'honeymoon' period of nationalisation – even if that honeymoon had been marked by some sharp marital differences.

One was the publication in May of the new Conservative Government's White Paper, *Transport Policy*. This began by stating, correctly enough, that integration of road and rail under the BTC had made little progress. But it went on to argue, with rather less justification, that the administration of the railways had become 'excessively centralised' and – with still less justification – that nationalised road haulage was unable to give proper service to industry and commerce.

It proposed, therefore, first to change the organisation of British Railways 'by giving greater autonomy to areas which may follow the general pattern of the present regions' to 'encourage a healthy rivalry between them'; second, to de-nationalise road haulage.

This meant the end of the Railway Executive and the end of road–rail 'integration'. The main reason for nationalisation, as it had been put forward by the Labour Government in 1946–7, was henceforth nullified. Yet railway de-nationalisation was not practicable or even considered.

The end of the beginning therefore came with ominous overtones for the future. The 1953 Transport Act did in fact abolish the Railway Executive – which was not wholly a disaster, though if that body had been reformed it could have fulfilled a useful role. The Act also initiated the de-nationalisation of road haulage, which proceeded some way and then ground to a stop because no more buyers were forthcoming. Neither measure really dealt with the growing problems of post-war transport. They were irrelevant, and based on purely political ideology.

Whilst the Conservative Party was still in opposition, I had been invited to attend an 'off the record' meeting to brief the then Shadow Minister of Transport about the real problems of the BTC. I had been disillusioned to discover that party policy had crystallised into the two largely irrelevant proposals outlined above. Road haulage was in fact beginning to confound the prophets by becoming quite efficient under nationalisation; and railways needed both a more progressive technical policy, such as emerged during the 1960s, and strong pressure to 'integrate' many of their services with road haulage on the lines of the Freightliner organisation that also emerged in the sixties. Had the 1953 Act dealt with these realities

TRANSPORT POLICY

Presented by the Minister of Transport to Parliament
by Command of Her Majesty
May 1952

LONDON
HER MAJESTY'S STATIONERY OFFICE
THREEPENCE NET

Cmd. 8538

56. A new era for British Railways: the Government decides to abolish the Railway Executive and to decentralise the railway management.

Crown Copyright

57. One of the few branch lines that did get closed long before Beeching; the last day of services on the Kelvedon–Tollesbury branch of the Eastern Region. Class J 69/1 0–6–0T no. 68578, based on Colchester shed, runs round its train at Tollesbury on 5 May 1951.

P. J. Lynch

instead of merely trying ineffectually to put the clock back the later difficulties of British Rail might have been much less acute.

Another sinister development took place in 1952. The Commission had submitted a passenger charges scheme to the Transport Tribunal, as required by the 1947 Act, and the Tribunal had confirmed the scheme though with some important modifications, reducing the standard single fare per mile. The Commission proposed – as they were entitled to do – to raise some sub-standard fares. But in March 1952 the Minister of Transport intervened and gave the BTC a statutory Direction to freeze all fares until he had decided on the treatment of sub-standard fares. This really marked the end of the period in which railway fares were still fixed without reference to political factors. From now on, the Minister was to be more and more involved in the finances of the railways – having set this precedent.

So far as freight charges were concerned, the 1947 Act had placed a duty on the BTC to introduce a charges scheme that would promote 'integration' of the various forms of nationalised transport. The Commission had to take the initiative, and it duly set up a Charges Committee upon which the Railway Executive was represented along with the Executives providing road and water transport. A great deal of preliminary work was done on the principles to be embodied in the scheme; for instance, origin and destination points were to be grouped under Ordnance Survey National Grid references, and the 'charging distances' were to be based upon the shortest road route. But there remained major differences of commercial philosophy to be

58. Sixty-five years of railway service ended in 1949 for coach no. 60462 on the Kelvedon–Tollesbury branch. It was built for the Wisbech and Upwell Tramway in 1884. The other coach, no. E62261, was built for the Denver and Stoke Ferry branch in 1896.

P. J. Lynch

resolved by the time that the Conservative Government took office in 1951 and indicated that so far as it was concerned integration was a dead duck. In future, as in due course the Transport Act, 1953 provided, charges schemes for the railways would be much more limited in scope and would in fact be quite close to the pre-war statutory control of railway rates, though with some relaxations.

In a sense, therefore, the years between nationalisation in 1948 and the second Transport Act in 1953 were wasted, in that virtually nothing was done to remodel freight rates so as to retain traffic in the face of growing road competition, particularly in the shape of increased use by traders of their own vehicles to carry their own goods over quite long distances. All that had happened was that the old system of freight rates set up by the Railways Act, 1921, including 'standard', 'exceptional' and 'agreed' charges, continued to apply, although to meet increased costs the Minister of Transport had authorised flat percentage increases of $16\frac{2}{3}$ per cent in May 1950, 10 per cent in April 1951 and 5 per cent in December 1952, as stopgap measures.

The Railway Executive cannot really be blamed for this waste of time; one Government had placed charges policy in the hands of the Commission, giving it a vast but ill-defined remit, and then, before the work could come to fruition, another Government brought the whole thing to a standstill.

However, the ultimately disastrous effects

of this chopping and changing of objectives were to manifest themselves only after 1953. Due largely to the lingering effects of post-war restrictions upon the supply of road vehicles and the continuation of motor fuel rationing, road competition had not begun to bite. During what may be called the financial honeymoon stage of nationalisation, the Executive had been able to show a surplus on railway working every year. The figures were:

	£ million
1948	26·3
1949	12·7
1950	26·3
1951	35·0
1952	39·6
1953	35·1

These may be roughly compared with £36·5 million, representing the average pre-war net earnings of the Railway Companies used as the basis for the guaranteed net revenue payable by the Government during the war control period. The comparison is not exact, as revenue from some 'ancillary businesses' is included in the pre-war but not the post-war figure. Equally, of course, money values were changing over the period. But it is clear enough that the railways were, broadly speaking, viable during the first stage of nationalisation.

Did nationalisation of itself help to achieve this result? The Railway Executive claimed to be effecting substantial economies from unification, though these were not very often quantified. Standard designs certainly led to a reduction in the number of items kept in stock, so that the reviews of varying Regional practices and standardising on the one which offered greatest economy and/or efficiency must have played a part. Resources, whether of rolling stock or locomotives or stocks of materials, were moved between Regions to even out surpluses and shortages, with consequent savings. Concentration of traffic upon freight terminals, closure of adjacent terminals, and

59. As late as 1950, the Great Western Stars were still on some main-line duties, although the class had been introduced by Churchward in 1907. Here, in BR livery and numbering, is no. 4036 leaving Reading for Paddington.

John Ashman FRPS

60. The glamour of a Coronation special train; a Pullman special, Dover Marine to Victoria, carrying foreign Heads of State to London for the coronation of HM the Queen, on 30 May 1953. The train is passing Wandsworth Road, in charge of Britannia class 4–6–2 no. 70004, 'William Shakespeare'.

S. C. Nash

reduction in town offices and canvassing all followed unification, thus extending the war-time co-operation between the Companies.

The Executive also closed some branch lines and stations; but this merely continued an activity that the Companies had pursued before the war, and the elimination of major duplicate routes was not tackled. The total mileage in fact fell only slightly over the period.

	Route-miles open for traffic
End of 1947	19,639
,, 1948	19,631
,, 1949	19,573
,, 1950	19,471
,, 1951	19,357
,, 1952	19,276
,, 1953	19,222

By comparison with the drastic scaling-down during the later Beeching era, the Railway Executive was merely nibbling at the edges of the unremunerative network.

After the first two or three years the Executive ceased, in the Annual Reports, to draw attention to the economies it was effecting through unification of top management. Many of them of course were of a once-and-for-all character. The Executive maintained consistently, however, that economies from standard practices and unified control could only be obtained through having direct 'functional' chains of command from members to departmental officers in the Regions, bypassing the Chief Regional Officers. That was possibly true. But it was partly the groundswell of Regional objections to dictation from 222 Marylebone Road that brought about the Executive's downfall. One must admit that increased Regional independence after 1953 was not an unmixed blessing; it was responsible for the unnecessary variation in traction policies and for some of the less justified elements of the £1,200 million Modernisation Plan of 1955.

The Executive's failures were threefold. It failed appreciably to improve staff productivity. Its traction policy was dominated by steam

61. As LMS as it is possible to be: a Midland Compound (though in BR livery and numbered 41124) arriving at Chester with a Liverpool train on 5 July 1952, passing under a gantry of typical London & North Western signals.

N. E. Preedy Collection

engineers. And in commercial policy, it failed to foresee the road transport explosion of the later 1950s and the 1960s. In the freight business in particular the policy was out of date, involving marshalling of wagons in concentration yards, and building only small containers. It failed to grasp the opportunity to press effective road–rail integration. In consequence, although the Executive complained every year that the investment permitted to it was quite inadequate, as indeed it was, much of the investment it did receive went into the wrong channels, from standard steam locomotives to short-wheelbase wagons and marshalling yards, and the old-fashioned Mark I coaching stock.

Having said this, one must ask whether nationalisation in 1948 was necessary, and how, if it had not taken place, the railways would have survived.

We have come to accept nationalised railways as the norm in this country, as they are in most other countries; we have also come to accept the need of the railways for deficit financing. These two factors are so closely associated in many people's minds that it is usually assumed that private railway Companies are impracticable, since they would inevitably be bankrupt. This is an oversimplification.

The railways in 1948 were very far from being bankrupt. They had certainly been overutilised and undermaintained during the war – due to Government requirements, so that railwaymen bitterly resented the sneer of Dr Dalton, Chancellor of the Exchequer, that the nation had purchased 'a poor bag of assets'. They had still in fact large liquid assets, which would have been much larger if the Government had allowed them during the war to operate commercially and retain the receipts from the swollen wartime traffic.

If railway nationalisation had not taken place in 1948, or subsequently, how in fact would the policies of the Companies have compared with what has actually taken place under the Railway Executive (1948–53), the British Transport Commission (1953–62) and the British Railways Board (1962 onwards)?

Obviously one must assume that a different Government had taken office in 1945. If so, the effect on the railways might have been on the following lines. First of all, diversification would have been pressed strongly forward. The railway Companies would have invested substantially in road haulage. Their ownership of Railway Air Services Ltd would have been exploited, as the report of the wartime Swinton Committee had recommended, to provide a network of internal air lines. The post-war boom in road travel would have yielded good returns

on the substantial railway shareholding in the major bus companies. Associated travel agencies such as Thomas Cook & Son would have been built up further.

The Companies had in 1939 already come to terms with the Road Haulage Association about future competition in a way that suggested that road and rail freight services could in future co-operate voluntarily, not by direction from above. I believe that the railways would have moved progressively towards becoming regional transport companies – just as the Southern Pacific Railroad in the USA has become the Southern Pacific Transportation Company.

The need to discard uneconomic operations would of course have existed and would indeed have been more keenly felt if there was no possibility of deficits being met by the Exchequer. I am sure that the costing of the less used lines and services would have proceeded steadily, but it would not have been a huge and sudden exercise like the Beeching 're-shaping', produced in a hurry under political pressure. The Companies would have started earlier and allowed themselves more time to study each case on its merits. They would, I believe, have operated their own bus services on an extensive scale to replace lightly used rail services. This would have been better than leaving the 'alternative service' provision to bus companies whose timetables and procedures are totally dissimilar to those of the railways.

So far as internal rationalisation and economies are concerned, the proposals of the Railway Companies Association Commission on Post-War Planning would largely have been implemented – including a separate railway organisation in Scotland, elimination of 'penetrating' and duplicate routes, and co-operation between the railways on technical research and

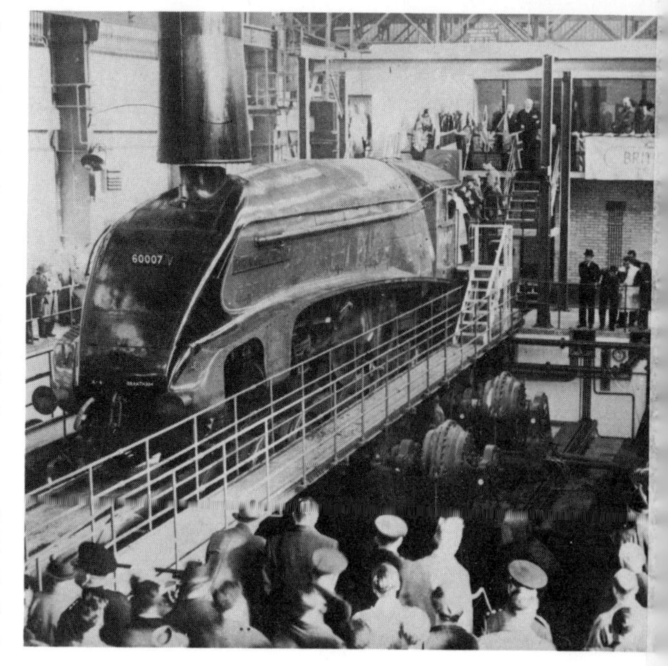

commercial policy – much, in other words, of what the Railway Executive did in the way of 'tidying-up' in this field. But I am confident that there would have been a more flexible and adventurous spirit abroad, and that there would have been less depression and cynicism among managers, arising from frequent and sometimes capricious changes of policy following reorganisation every few years.

It would be wrong to paint too rosy a picture. It may well be that nothing could have completely averted the massive movement of the 1950s and 1960s away from public transport, eventually involving support from public funds for the latter if it was not to close down completely. One cannot say. But one thing is quite clear: nationalisation in 1948 may have been a political necessity; it was not at that time an economic necessity. There was great tenacity in the private railway Companies and a will to survive in a competitive world.

62. Steam's Indian Summer was to be a short one. But this was not suspected when the Rugby Locomotive Testing Station was opened on 19 October 1948. As a graceful tribute to a great designer, the first locomotive to be run on the test bed is the A4 Pacific, now renumbered 60007, 'Sir Nigel Gresley'.

National Railway Museum

A Note on Sources

For the political background to nationalisation, four documents are important. They are:

Labour Party Election Manifesto (1945): *Let Us Face the Future*;
Pamphlet by Herbert Morrison: *British Transport at Britain's Service*;
Pamphlet by the Trades Union Congress: *The Public Operation of Transport*;
Pamphlet by the Railway Clerks Association: *On the Way to Greater Service.*

The principal study of the process is contained in Sir Norman Chaster's monumental *The Nationalisation of British Industry, 1945–51.*

A shorter, critical study is R. Kelf-Cohen, *Twenty Years of Nationalisation*. Organisation questions are dealt with in my own *The Organisation of British Railways* (1971).

Official papers including those of the Cabinet and the Ministry of Transport are now available in the Public Record Office; the minutes and other papers of the British Transport Commission and the Railway Executive are also available by permission.

Reasons for the decision to abolish the Railway Executive are given in the Government's White Paper *Transport Policy* (Cmd. 8538) of May 1952.

The Annual Reports of the British Transport Commission (including a section for the Railway Executive) are very full and informative over the period 1948–53.

A short account of the post-nationalisation years is contained in *Rail 150* published by the British Railways Board.

For the train services and locomotive history of the period, the *Railway Gazette* and *Railway Magazine* files are invaluable. So are the *Scrapbooks* for individual years published by Ian Allan Ltd. Traction policy has produced many books, polemical, autobiographical and nostalgic. The best informed and most unbiased account is by E. S. Cox: *Locomotive Panorama*.

Other books covering the period with varying degrees of objectivity include D. H. Aldcroft, *British Railways in Transition*; G. F. Fiennes, *I Tried to Run a Railway*; A. J. Pearson, *Man of the Rail.*

The problems of nationalised transport have been the subject of major studies by economists such as A. M. Milne, C. D. Foster, K. Gwilliam and J. M. Thomson; but their attention has been chiefly concentrated upon the period after 1953, and the conflict between the 'service' and the 'industry' character of the railways after working deficits had appeared.

Index

Accidents:
  Abington (Sc.R) 83
  Ardler Jct. (Sc.R) 79
  Beattock (Sc.R) 80
  Blea Moor (LMR) 83
  Doncaster (ER) 81
  s.s. *Duke of York* 83, 94
  East Coast floods (Sc.R) 78
  Ford (SR) 81
  Guildford (SR) 84
  Harrow (LMR) 81
  Huntingdon (ER) 80
  Manchester (LMR) 83
  Newcastle (NER) 81
  New Southgate (ER) 78
  Penmaenmawr (LMR) 80
  Penmanshiel (Sc.R) 80
  Polesworth (LMR) 81
  m.v. *Princess Victoria* 83, 94
  Stockport (LMR) 79
  Wath Road (LMR) 78
  Weedon (LMR) 81
  Winsford (LMR) 78
Allen, W. P. 28
Ashfield, Lord 23, 25, 26
Associated Society of Locomotive Engineers and Firemen (ASLEF) 87
Atchison Topeka and Santa Fe RR 96
Automatic Train Control 84, 85

Bain, David 70
Barnes, Rt Hon. Alfred 17, 18, 23
Barrington-Ward, V. M. (Sir Michael) 28
Beeching, Dr R. (Lord) 23, 102, 104
Beevor, Miles 25
Benstead, (Sir) John 23, 25, 86
Bird, C. K. 33
Blee, David 28, 37
British Railways Board 11, 93
British Transport Commission:
  name on notice boards 14
  powers and duties 18, 21, 30
  membership 23, 64, 86
  relations with Railway Executive 21, 25, 30, 31, 36, 39, 41
  motive power policy 53, 64, 68
  approval of electrification scheme 60
  views on 'tavern' cars 75
  modernisation plan (1955) 77, 85
  annual report (accidents) 81
  views on A.T.C. 84
  joint consultation with Unions 86, 87
  pensions scheme for wages grades 89
  central activities 54, 91
  common services for executives 92
  earnings from RE ships 94
  passenger Charges Scheme 99, 100
Bulleid, Oliver 54, 55, 57, 74

Caledonian Railway 71
Cameron, T. F. 37
Carriages:
  Company designs 70, 71
  BR standard designs 73
  'tavern' cars 74, 75
  government restrictions on building 75
Carter Paterson Ltd 91
Churchward, G. J. 54
Clayton, David 70
Collett, C. B. 54
Conservative Party policy 21, 97, 100

Cook, Kenneth 55
Cook (Thos) & Son Ltd 91, 104
Coras Iompair Eireann 55
Cox, E. S. 53, 55, 57

Dalton, Dr Hugh 103
Darbyshire, G. L. 35
Dean and Dawson Ltd 91
Diesel traction (see also locomotives):
  LNER East Coast scheme 39
  GN Main Line scheme 59
  Railway Executive policy 60, 69
  multiple-units 64, 68
Docks and Inland Waterways Executive 91

Eastern Region 32, 33, 46, 55, 60, 61, 78, 94
Electrification:
  Southern Railway plans 39, 61
  GN Main Line proposal 59
  Railway Executive policy 60
  Eastern Region projects 60, 61, 62
  Lancaster/Morecambe/Heysham experiment 63
Elliot, J. B. (Sir John) 35, 36, 37

Fairburn, C. E. 54
Fay, Sir Sam 26
Fell, Lt-Col 63
Figgins, J. 23
Frederick Hotels Ltd 96
Freightliners 97

Gas turbines – see Locomotives
Gladstone's Cheap Trains Act (1844) 15
Grand, K. W. C. 37
Great Central Hotel 26
Great Central Railway 26, 34
Great Eastern Railway 34
Great Northern Railway 34
Great Western Railway 41, 54, 63, 64, 70, 84
Gresley, Sir Nigel 54, 70

Harrington, J. L. 58
Harrison, J. F. 55
Harvey, Fred 96
Hawksworth, F. W. 54, 55
Hay's Wharf Cartage Co. 91
Hopkins, C. P. 34, 35, 37
Hotels Executive 94, 96
Hotels, railway:
  LMS and LNER compared 94
  transfer to Hotels Executive 94
Hudson, George 33
Hurcomb, Sir Cyril (Lord) 17, 23, 25, 26, 31, 44, 52, 53, 84
Hyde, Walter 34

Industrial disputes 87, 88
Ivatt, H. G. 54, 55

Jones, C. M. Jenkin 34

Labour Party (and nationalisation) 15, 86, 93, 97
Lloyd George, D. (Lord) 87
Locomotives (diesel):
  LMS and SR prototypes 39, 63
  'Fell' experimental design 63
  827 h.p. prototype 63

Locomotives (gas turbine) 39
Locomotives (steam):
Company designs 55, 57
exchange trials, 1948 52
BR standard designs 52, 53, 55, 58, 69
London Midland Region 31, 35, 36, 37, 46, 48, 55, 58, 63, 78, 79, 80, 81, 94
London Midland and Scottish Railway 22, 32, 33, 34, 37, 39, 54, 58, 63, 70, 73, 84, 85, 90, 94
London and North Eastern Railway 26, 32, 33, 34, 37, 39, 46, 54, 58, 60, 63, 70, 81, 90, 92, 94, 96
London and North Western Railway 35, 70, 71
London Transport Executive 15, 63, 92

Maple, Sir Blundell 26
Maunsell, R. E. L. 54, 70
Midland Railway 34, 35, 42, 70, 71, 94
Milne, Sir James 23, 28
Missenden, Sir Eustace 28, 30, 31, 58
Morrison, Herbert (Lord) 15, 17, 18

National Carriers Ltd 93
National Freight Corporation 93
National Union of Railwaymen (NUR) 23, 87, 96
Nationalisation – *see under* Labour Party, Conservative Party, Transport Bill, Transport Act, British Transport Commission, Railway Executive
North British Railway 78
North Eastern Railway 78, 90
North Eastern Region 32, 46, 55, 81, 94
North Western Region (proposed) 37

Park C. A. 71
Pensions, railway 89
Peppercorn, A. H. 54, 55
Pick, Frank 26
Pickfords Ltd 91
Pope, F. A. 64, 68
Pullman Car Company Ltd 37, 96

Railway Air Services Ltd 92, 103
Railway Benevolent Institution 89
Railway Clerks Association 87
Railway Companies Association 39, 104
Railway Convalescent Homes 89
Railway Executive, The:
legal title 13
name on notice boards 14
relations with BTC 21, 25, 30, 31, 36, 39, 41
powers and duties 21
headquarters office 26, 28
membership 28, 37, 86
regions 31, 32, 41
attitude to Company plans 39
locomotive and train liveries 42, 44
totem 46
steam traction policy 52, 53
relations with ex-CMEs 55
Committee on Types of Motive Power 58, 59, 60
electrification policy 61, 63
diesel traction policy 63, 64, 68
carriage building policy 73, 74
'tavern' cars 74, 75
Ideal Stocks Committee 75

wagon building policy 76, 77
attitude to A.T.C. 84, 85
employer of staff 86
Joint Advisory Council for Welfare 87
staff numbers 88, 89
traffic apprenticeship scheme 90
ancillary businesses 91, 93
opposes BTC common services 92
shipping services results 94
abolition (forecast) 97
Charges Committee membership 99
delay in authority to raise rates 100
achievement of surpluses 101
unification economies 101
unremunerative services 102
investment ceilings 103
Railway Executive Committee 21
Richards, H. W. H. 39
Riddles, R. A. 28, 58, 68, 73
Road Haulage Association 104
Road Haulage Executive 30, 91
Road Transport Executive 30, 91
Robertson, Sir Brian (Lord) 23, 44
Rusholme, Lord 23, 25

Schools, railway 90
Scottish Region 37, 46, 48, 79
Ships:
s.s. *Amsterdam* 93
s.s. *Brighton* 93
m.v. *Cambria* 93
s.s. *Duke of York* 83, 94
m.v. *Hibernia* 93
s.s. *Lord Warden* 94
s.s. *Maid of Orleans* 93
m.v. *Norfolk Ferry* 94
s.s. *Normannia* 94
m.v. *Princess Victoria* 83, 94
Short, H. A. 37
Slim, Sir William (Lord) 28
Southern Pacific RR 104
Southern Pacific Transportation Co. 104
Southern Railway 39, 42, 61, 63, 70, 90, 96
Southern Region 32, 35, 37, 42, 46, 50, 55, 57, 81, 84, 85, 94, 96
Spiers and Pond Ltd 96
'Square Deal' campaign 17, 22
Stamp, Lord 23, 26
Stanier, Sir William 54, 58
Swinton Committee 103

'Tavern' cars 74, 75
Thompson, Edward 54, 55, 57
Tilling Group 91
Traffic Apprenticeships 90
Train, J. C. L. (Sir Landale) 28
Trains (named):
'Atlantic Coast Express' 50
'Bon Accord' 48
'Capitals Limited' 47
'Cheltenham Flier' 51
'Comet' 48
'Cornish Riviera Express' 50
'Coronation' 47
'Devon Belle' 50
'Elizabethan' 47
'Golden Arrow' 50
'Granite City' 48
'Irish Mail' (accident) 80
'Irishman' 48
'Man of Kent' 50

'Master Cutler' 47
'Merchant Venturer' 51
'Merseyside Express' 48
'North Briton' 47
'Pembroke Coast Express' 51
'Queen of Scots' 48
'Red Dragon' 51
'Royal Scot' 48
'St Mungo' 48
'South Yorkshireman' 47
'Tees-Tyne Pullman' 47
'Thames-Clyde Express' (accident) 83
'Thanet Belle' 50
'Torbay Express' 50
Transport Act, 1947 14, 18
Transport Act, 1953 97, 98
Transport Bill, 1946 18, 21
Transport Salaried Staffs Association 87

Ulster Transport Authority 64

Wages, railway 87
Wagon Building policy 75, 76
Walker, Sir Herbert 23, 31, 32, 70
Warder, S. B. 55
Warner, Surrey 70
Watkins, J. W. 36
Watson, Sir Daril 28
Wedgwood, Sir Ralph 23, 26
Western Region 37, 39, 41, 46, 50, 51, 94
Wilson, R. H. (Sir Reginald) 25
Wood, Sir William 22, 23, 25, 26, 35
Workshops, railway 55, 57, 93

17/8
26